HE STILL
MOVES
STONES

HE STILL MOVES STONES

MAX LUCADO

WORD PUBLISHING
Dallas·London·Vancouver·Melbourne

HE STILL MOVES STONES

Unless otherwise indicated, all Scripture references are from the New Century Version of the Bible, copyright © 1987, 1988, 1991, Word Publishing. Other Scripture quotations are from:

The New King James Version (NKJV), copyright © 1979, 1980, 1982, Thomas Nelson, Inc., Publisher.

The Holy Bible, New International Version (NIV), copyright © 1973, 1978, 1984 International Bible Society, and are used by permission of Zondervan Bible Publishers.

The Living Bible (TLB), copyright © 1971 by Tyndale House Publishers, Wheaton, Ill. Used by permission.

The New Testament in Modern English by J. B. Phillips (PHILLIPS), published by The Macmillan Company, © 1958, 1960, 1972 by J. B. Phillips.

Library of Congress Cataloging-in-Publication Data is available.

ISBN 0–8499–0864–7   LC 93–14512

Printed in the United States of America

For the Oak Hills Family

May we continue to grow together,
and together may we continue to grow.

Contents

Acknowledgments

Writing a book and traversing a desert have much in common. Long stretches of dry flatland marked with occasional pools of inspiration. Here's a salute to dear friends who made this journey so pleasant. Thanks for not complaining at the sand and celebrating at each oasis.

For my assistant, Karen Hill: You do more than organize my office and edit my writing. You preserve my sanity!

For my editor, Liz Heaney: Like a good surgeon, your judgment is keen and your scalpel sharp.

For the family at Word Publishing: To each of you—editors, artists, secretaries, receptionists, salespeople, and decision makers—you're the best.

For Roy and Barbie Johnston: Thanks for loaning me your Horseshoe Bay hideaway.

For UpWords Executive Director Steve Green: No one else could do what you do the way you do it. We are in your debt.

For my wife, Denalyn: What else can I say? You are starlight and I'm Galileo. Your sparkle still stuns.

And for you the reader, I reserve my final salute:

For some of you this book marks our tenth encounter (happy anniversary!). For others it's our first (glad to meet you). And for most, this is somewhere in between (good to be with you again).

You are about to entrust me with your most valuable asset—your time. I pledge to be a good steward. Though writing a book can be like a desert journey, reading a book shouldn't be. It should be a pause at the oasis. I hope it is.

Drink deeply.

Max Lucado

1

BRUISED REEDS AND SMOLDERING WICKS

A bruised reed he will not break,
and a smoldering wick he will not
snuff out.

Matthew 12:20 NIV

---

*I*magine it's a Saturday afternoon in October. What you needed to get done today, you've already done. Your afternoon lies before you with no obligations. Free afternoons don't come as often as they once did, so you consider your options for the day. You pick up a paper to get some ideas. A movie? Nothing good is showing. Television? You can do that any time. Wait. What's this? An ad catches your eye.

Special Art Exhibit
"Bruised Reeds and Smoldering Wicks"
2:00 to 4:00 Saturday Afternoon
Lincoln Library

Hmm . . . It's been a while since you've seen some good art. Bruised Reeds and Smoldering Wicks? Probably some nature stuff. Besides, the walk would be nice. You'll do it. You lay down the paper, put on a coat, and grab some gloves.

You're greeted by the musty odor of books as you walk through the library doors. Behind the counter sits a librarian with her hair in a bun and a pencil behind her ear. A student with a backpack at his feet stares into a drawer of cataloged cards. A table featuring old *Life* magazines strikes you as interesting. You start to pick up the one with Truman on the cover when you see

13

a sign that reminds you why you came. "Bruised Reeds and Smoldering Wicks" it reads and points you toward a door. You walk across a hallway and open one of two heavy, wooden doors and step in.

It's an intimate room—no larger than a nice den. Bookshelves cover the walls, and books line the shelves. A fire crackles in a fireplace, and a couple of high wingback chairs invite you to spend the afternoon with a good book. *Maybe later,* you think. *First, the art.*

Placed around the room are the paintings. All framed. All in vivid color. All set on easels, in pairs, and always back to back. You put your gloves in your coat pocket, hang your coat on a hook, and move toward the first painting.

It's a portrait of a leper, the center figure on the canvas. He stoops like a hunchback. His fingerless hand, draped in rags, extends toward you, pleading. A tattered wrap hides all of his face except two pain-filled eyes. The crowd around the leper is chaotic. A father is grabbing a curious child. A woman trips over her own feet as she scrambles to get away. A man glares over his shoulder as he runs. The painting is entitled with the leper's plea, "If you will, you can . . ."

The next painting portrays the same leper, but the scene has changed dramatically. The title has only two words, "I will." In this sketch the leper is standing erect and tall. He is looking at his own outstretched hand—it has fingers! The veil is gone from his face and he is smiling. There is no crowd; only one other person is standing beside the leper. You can't see his face, but you can see his hand on the shoulder of the healed man.

"This is no nature exhibit," you whisper to yourself as you turn to the next painting.

In this one the artist's brush has captured a woman in mid-air, jumping from one side of a canyon to another. Her clothes are ragged. Her body is frail, and her skin is pale. She looks anemic. Her eyes are desperate as she reaches for the canyon wall with both hands. On the ledge is a man. All you see are his legs, sandals, and the hem of a robe. Beneath the painting are the woman's words, "If only . . ."

You step quickly to see the next scene. She is standing now. The ground beneath her bare feet is solid. Her face flushes with life. Her cautious eyes look up at the half-moon of people that surround her. Standing beside her is the one she sought to touch. The caption? His words. "Take heart . . ."

The next portrait is surrealistic. A man's contorted face dominates the canvas. Orange hair twists against a purple background. The face stretches downward and swells at the bottom like a pear. The eyes are perpendicular slits in which a thousand tiny pupils bounce. The mouth is frozen open in a scream. You notice something odd—it's inhabited! Hundreds of spiderish creatures claw over each other. Their desperate voices are captured by the caption, "Swear to God you won't torture me!"

Fascinated, you step to the next painting. It is the same man, but now his features are composed. His eyes, no longer wild, are round and soft. The mouth is closed, and the caption explains the sudden peace: "Released." The man is leaning forward as if listening intently. His hand strokes his chin. And dangling from his wrist is a shackle and a chain—a broken chain.

In another portrait a scantily clothed female cowers before an angry mob of men who threaten her with stones. In the next painting the stones lie harmlessly on the ground, littering the courtyard occupied by a surprised woman and a smiling man who stands over some pictures drawn in the dirt.

In one painting a paralytic on a pallet urges his friends not to give up as they stare at a house overflowing with people. In the next the pallet is on the boy's shoulders as he skips out the door of the house.

In one picture a blind man screams to a rabbi. In the next he bows before the one to whom he screamed.

Throughout the gallery the sequence repeats itself. Always two paintings, one of a person in trauma and one of a person in peace. "Before" and "after" testimonials to a life-changing encounter. Scene after scene of serenity eclipsing sorrow. Purpose defeating pain. Hope outshining hurt.

But alone in the center of the hall is a single painting. It is different from the others. There are no faces. No people. The artist has dipped his brush into ancient prophecy and sketched two simple objects—a reed and a wick.

> A bruised reed he will not break,
>   and a smoldering wick he will not snuff out.
>
> Matthew 12:20 NIV

Is there anything more frail than a bruised reed? Look at the bruised reed at the water's edge. A once slender and tall stalk of sturdy river grass, it is now bowed and bent.

Are you a bruised reed? Was it so long ago that you stood so tall, so proud? You were upright and sturdy, nourished by the waters and rooted in the riverbed of confidence.

Then something happened. You were bruised . . .

by harsh words
by a friend's anger
by a spouse's betrayal
by your own failure
by religion's rigidity.

And you were wounded, bent ever so slightly. Your hollow reed, once erect, now stooped, and hidden in the bulrush.

And the smoldering wick on the candle. Is there anything closer to death than a smoldering wick? Once aflame, now flickering and failing. Still warm from yesterday's passion, but no fire. Not yet cold but far from hot. Was it that long ago you blazed with faith? Remember how you illuminated the path?

Then came the wind . . . the cold wind, the harsh wind. They said your ideas were foolish. They told you your dreams were too lofty. They scolded you for challenging the time-tested.

The constant wind wore down upon you. Oh, you stood strong for a moment (or maybe a lifetime), but the endless blast whipped your flickering flame, leaving you one pinch away from darkness.

The bruised reed and the smoldering wick. Society knows what to do with you. The world has a place for the beaten. The world will break you off; the world will snuff you out.

But the artists of Scripture proclaim that God won't. Painted on canvas after canvas is the tender touch of a Creator who has a special place for the bruised and weary of the world. A God who is the friend of the wounded heart. A God who is the keeper of your dreams. That's the theme of the New Testament.

And that's the theme of the gallery.

Let's stroll through the gallery together. Let's ponder the moments when Christ met people at their points of pain. We'll see the prophecy proved true. We'll see bruised reeds straightened and smoldering wicks ignited.

It's quite a collection of paintings. By the way, your portrait is in the gallery too. Go ahead. Look at it. It's there, to the side. Just like the others, there are two easels. But unlike the others, these canvases are white. Your name is at the bottom. Beside the easel is a table with paint and a brush . . .

THE BRUISED REED

It stood with assurance.
Head held high on strong stalk.
But that was before the careless bump, the harsh rain.
Now it's bruised, bent. Weakened.
It seeks gentle fingers to straighten and not break.
It needs a firm touch to heal and not to hurt.
Tender power.
Soft strength.
Is there such a hand?

2

NOT GUILTY

Overcoming Shame

Jesus went to the Mount of Olives. But early in the morning he went back to the Temple, and all the people came to him, and he sat and taught them. The teachers of the law and the Pharisees brought a woman who had been caught in adultery. They forced her to stand before the people. They said to Jesus, "Teacher, this woman was caught having sexual relations with a man who is not her husband. The law of Moses commands that we stone to death every woman who does this. What do you say we should do?" They were asking this to trick Jesus so that they could have some charge against him.

But Jesus bent over and started writing on the ground with his finger. When they continued to ask Jesus their question, he raised up and said, "Anyone here who has never sinned can throw the first stone at her." Then Jesus bent over again and wrote on the ground.

Those who heard Jesus began to leave one by one, first the older men and then the others. Jesus was left there alone with the woman standing before him. Jesus raised up again and asked her, "Woman, where are they? Has no one judged you guilty?"

She answered, "No one, sir."

Then Jesus said, "I also don't judge you guilty. You may go now, but don't sin anymore."

John 8:1–11

Rebecca Thompson fell twice from the Fremont Canyon Bridge. She died both times. The first fall broke her heart; the second broke her neck.

She was only eighteen years of age when she and her eleven-year-old sister were abducted by a pair of hoodlums near a store in Casper, Wyoming. They drove the girls forty miles southwest to the Fremont Canyon Bridge, a one-lane, steel-beamed structure rising 112 feet above the North Platte River.

The men brutally beat and raped Rebecca. She somehow convinced them not to do the same to her sister Amy. Both were thrown over the bridge into the narrow gorge. Amy died when she landed on a rock near the river, but Rebecca slammed into a ledge and was ricocheted into deeper water.

With a hip fractured in five places, she struggled to the shore. To protect her body from the cold, she wedged herself between two rocks and waited until the dawn.

But the dawn never came for Rebecca. Oh, the sun came up, and she was found. The physicians treated her wounds, and the courts imprisoned her attackers. Life continued, but the dawn never came.

The blackness of her night of horrors lingered. She was never able to climb out of the canyon. So in September 1992, nineteen years later, she returned to the bridge.

23

Against her boyfriend's pleadings, she drove seventy miles-per-hour to the North Platte River. With her two-year-old daughter and boyfriend at her side, she sat on the edge of the Fremont Canyon Bridge and wept. Through her tears she retold the story. The boyfriend didn't want the child to see her mother cry, so he carried the toddler to the car.

That's when he heard her body hit the water.

And that's when Rebecca Thompson died her second death. The sun never dawned on Rebecca's dark night. Why? What eclipsed the light from her world?

Fear? Perhaps. She had testified against the men, pointing them out in the courtroom. One of the murderers had taunted her by smirking and sliding his finger across his throat. On the day of her death, the two had been up for parole. Perhaps the fear of a second encounter was too great.

Was it anger? Anger at her rapists? Anger at the parole board? Anger at herself for the thousand falls in the thousand nightmares that followed? Or anger at God for a canyon that grew ever deeper and a night that grew ever blacker and a dawn that never came?

Was it guilt? Some think so. Despite Rebecca's attractive smile and appealing personality, friends say that she struggled with the ugly fact that she had survived and her little sister had not.

Was it shame? Everyone she knew and thousands she didn't had heard the humiliating details of her tragedy. The stigma was tattooed deeper with the newspaper ink of every headline. She had been raped. She had been violated. She had been shamed. And try as she might to outlive and outrun the memory . . . she never could.

So nineteen years later she went back to the bridge.

Canyons of shame run deep. Gorges of never-ending guilt. Walls ribboned with the greens and grays of death. Unending echoes of screams. Put your hands over your ears. Splash water on your face. Stop looking over your shoulder. Try as you might to outrun yesterday's tragedies—their tentacles are longer than your hope. They draw you back to the bridge of sorrows to be shamed again and again and again.

If it was your fault, it would be different. If you were to blame, you could apologize. If the tumble into the canyon was your mistake, you could respond. But you weren't a volunteer. You were a victim.

Sometimes your shame is private. Pushed over the edge by an abusive spouse. Molested by a perverted parent. Seduced by a compromising superior. No one else knows. But you know. And that's enough.

Sometimes it's public. Branded by a divorce you didn't want. Contaminated by a disease you never expected. Marked by a handicap you didn't create. And whether it's actually in their eyes or just in your imagination, you have to deal with it—you are marked: a divorcee, an invalid, an orphan, an AIDS patient.

Whether private or public, shame is always painful. And unless you deal with it, it is permanent. Unless you get help— the dawn will never come.

You're not surprised when I say there are Rebecca Thompsons in every city and Fremont Bridges in every town. And there are many Rebecca Thompsons in the Bible. So many, in fact, that it almost seems that the pages of Scripture are stitched together with their stories. You've met many in this book. Each acquainted with the hard floor of the canyon of shame.

But there is one woman whose story embodies them all. A story of failure. A story of abuse. A story of shame.

And a story of grace.

That's her, the woman standing in the center of the circle. Those men around her are religious leaders. Pharisees, they are called. Self-appointed custodians of conduct. And the other man, the one in the simple clothes, the one sitting on the ground, the one looking at the face of the woman, that's Jesus.

Jesus has been teaching.

The woman has been cheating.

And the Pharisees are out to stop them both.

"Teacher, this woman was caught in the act of adultery" (John 8:4 NIV). The accusation rings off the courtyard walls.

"Caught in the act of adultery." The words alone are enough to make you blush. Doors slammed open. Covers jerked back.

"In the act." In the arms. In the moment. In the embrace.

"Caught." Aha! What have we here? This man is not your husband. Put on some clothes! We know what to do with women like you!

In an instant she is yanked from private passion to public spectacle. Heads poke out of windows as the posse pushes her through the streets. Dogs bark. Neighbors turn. The city sees. Clutching a thin robe around her shoulders, she hides her nakedness.

But nothing can hide her shame.

From this second on, she'll be known as an adulteress. When she goes to the market, women will whisper. When she passes, heads will turn. When her name is mentioned, the people will remember.

Moral failure finds easy recall.

The greater travesty, however, goes unnoticed. What the woman did is shameful, but what the Pharisees did is despicable. According to the law, adultery was punishable by death, but only if two people witnessed the act. There had to be two eyewitnesses.

Question: How likely are two people to be eyewitnesses to adultery? What are the chances of two people stumbling upon an early morning flurry of forbidden embraces? Unlikely. But if you do, odds are it's not a coincidence.

So we wonder. How long did the men peer through the window before they barged in? How long did they lurk behind the curtain before they stepped out?

And what of the man? Adultery requires two participants. What happened to him? Could it be that he slipped out?

The evidence leaves little doubt. It was a trap. She's been caught. But she'll soon see that she is not the catch—she's only the bait.

"The law of Moses commands that we stone to death every woman who does this. What do you say we should do?" (v. 5).

Pretty cocky, this committee of high ethics. Pretty proud of themselves, these agents of righteousness. This will be a moment they long remember, the morning they foil and snag the mighty Nazarene.

As for the woman? Why, she's immaterial. Merely a pawn in their game. Her future? It's unimportant. Her reputation? Who cares if it's ruined? She is a necessary, yet dispensable, part of their plan.

The woman stares at the ground. Her sweaty hair dangles. Her tears drip hot with hurt. Her lips are tight, her jaw is clenched. She knows she's been framed. No need to look up. She'll find no kindness. She looks at the stones in their hands. Squeezed so tightly that fingertips turn white.

She thinks of running. But where? She could claim mistreatment. But to whom? She could deny the act, but she was seen. She could beg for mercy, but these men offer none.

The woman has nowhere to turn.

You'd expect Jesus to stand and proclaim judgment on the hypocrites. He doesn't. You'd hope that he would snatch the woman and the two would be beamed to Galilee. That's not what happens either. You'd imagine that an angel would descend or heaven would speak or the earth would shake. No, none of that.

Once again, his move is subtle.

But, once again, his message is unmistakable.

What does Jesus do? (If you already know, pretend you don't and feel the surprise.)

Jesus writes in the sand.

He stoops down and draws in the dirt. The same finger that engraved the commandments on Sinai's peak and seared the warning on Belshazzar's wall now scribbles in the courtyard floor. And as he writes, he speaks: "Anyone here who has never sinned can throw the first stone at her" (v. 7).

The young look to the old. The old look in their hearts. They are the first to drop their stones. And as they turn to leave, the young who were cocky with borrowed convictions do the same. The only sound is the thud of rocks and the shuffle of feet.

Jesus and the woman are left alone. With the jury gone, the courtroom becomes the judge's chambers, and the woman awaits his verdict. *Surely, a sermon is brewing. No doubt, he's going to demand that I apologize.* But the judge doesn't speak. His head is down, perhaps he's still writing in the sand. He seems surprised when he realizes that she is still there.

"Woman, where are they? Has no one judged you guilty?"

She answers, "No one, sir."

Then Jesus says, "I also don't judge you guilty. You may go now, but don't sin anymore" (vv. 10–11).

If you have ever wondered how God reacts when you fail, frame these words and hang them on the wall. Read them. Ponder them. Drink from them. Stand below them and let them wash over your soul.

Or better still, take him with you to your canyon of shame. Invite Christ to journey with you back to the Fremont Bridge of your world. Let him stand beside you as you retell the events of the darkest nights of your soul.

And then listen. Listen carefully. He's speaking.

"I don't judge you guilty."

And watch. Watch carefully. He's writing. He's leaving a message. Not in the sand, but on a cross.

Not with his hand, but with his blood.

His message has two words: Not guilty.

3

DON'T MISS THE PARTY

The Dungeon of the Bitter

"The older son was in the field, and as he came closer to the house, he heard the sound of music and dancing. So he called to one of the servants and asked what all this meant. The servant said, 'Your brother has come back, and your father killed the fat calf, because your brother came home safely.' The older son was angry and would not go in to the feast. So his father went out and begged him to come in. But the older son said to his father, 'I have served you like a slave for many years and have always obeyed your commands. But you never gave me even a young goat to have at a feast with my friends. But your other son, who wasted all your money on prostitutes, comes home, and you kill the fat calf for him!' The father said to him, 'Son, you are always with me, and all that I have is yours. We had to celebrate and be happy because your brother was dead, but now he is alive. He was lost, but now he is found.'"

Luke 15:25–32

> "The older son was angry and would
> not go in to the feast."
>
> Luke 15:28

$\mathcal{T}$he case of the elder brother.

A difficult one because he looked so good. He kept his room straight and his nose clean. He played by the rules and paid all his dues. His résumé? Impeccable. His credit? Squeaky clean. And loyalty? While his brother was sowing wild oats, he stayed home and sowed the crops.

On the outside he was everything a father could want in a son. But on the inside he was sour and hollow. Overcome by jealousy. Consumed by anger. Blinded by bitterness.

You remember the story. It's perhaps the best known of all the parables Jesus told. It's the third of three stories in Luke 15, three stories of three parties.

The first began after a shepherd found a sheep he'd lost. He had ninety-nine others. He could have been content to write this one off as a loss. But shepherds don't think like businessmen. So he searched for it. When he found the sheep, he carried it back to the flock, cut the best grass for the sheep to eat, and had a party to celebrate.

The second party was held in front of a house. A housewife had lost a coin. It wasn't her only coin, but you would have thought it was by the way she acted. She moved the furniture, got out the dust mop, and swept the whole house till she found it. And when she did, she ran shouting into the cul-de-sac and invited her neighbors over for a party to celebrate.

Then there is the story of the lost son. The boy who broke his father's heart by taking his inheritance and taking off. He trades his dignity for a whisky bottle and his self-respect for a pigpen. Then comes the son's sorrow and his decision to go home. He hopes his dad will give him a job on the farm and an apartment over the garage. What he finds is a father who has kept his absent son's place set at the table and the porch light on every night.

The father is so excited to see his son, you'll never guess what he does. That's right! He throws a party! We party-loving prodigals love what he did, but it infuriated the elder brother.

"The older son was angry" (v. 28). It's not hard to see why. "So, is this how a guy gets recognition in this family? Get drunk and go broke and you get a party?" So he sat outside the house and pouted.

I did that once. I pouted at a party. A Christmas party. I was in the fourth grade. Fourth graders take parties very seriously, especially when there are gifts involved. We had drawn names. Since you didn't know who had your name, you had to drop your hints very loudly. I didn't miss a chance. I wanted a "Sixth Finger"—a toy pistol that fit in the cleft of your hand and looked like a finger. (Honestly, it did exist!)

Finally the day came to open the gifts. I just knew I was going to get my pistol. Everyone in the class had heard my hints. I tore into the wrapping and ripped open the box and . . . know what I got? Stationery. Western stationery. Paper and envelopes with horses in the corners. Yuck! Probably left over from the Christmas before. Ten-year-old boys don't write letters! What was this person thinking? No doubt some mom forgot all about the present until this morning, so she went to the closet and rumbled about until she came out with stationery.

Tie my hands and feet and throw me in the river. I was distraught. I was upset. So I missed the party. I was present, but I pouted.

So did the big brother. He, too, felt he was a victim of inequity. When his father came out to meet him, the son started at the top, listing the atrocities of his life. To hear him say it, his woes began the day he was born.

"I have served you like a slave for many years and have always obeyed your commands. But you never gave me even a young goat to have at a feast with my friends. But your other son, who wasted all your money on prostitutes, comes home, and you kill the fat calf for him!" (v. 29–30).

Appears that both sons spent time in the pigpen. One in the pen of rebellion—the other in the pen of self-pity. The younger one has come home. The older one hasn't. He's still in the slop. He is saying the same thing you said when the kid down the street got a bicycle and you didn't. It's not fair!

That's what Wanda Holloway of Channelview, Texas, said. When it looked like her fourteen-year-old daughter wouldn't get elected to the cheerleading squad, Wanda got angry. She decided to get even. She hired a hit man to kill the mother of her daughter's chief competitor, hoping to so upset the girl that Wanda's daughter would make the squad. Bitterness will do that to you. It'll cause you to burn down your house to kill a rat.

Fortunately, her plan failed and Wanda Holloway was caught. She was sentenced to fifteen years. She didn't have to be put behind bars to be imprisoned, however. Bitterness is its own prison.

Black and cold, bitterness denies easy escape. The sides are slippery with resentment. A floor of muddy anger stills the feet. The stench of betrayal fills the air and stings the eyes. A cloud of self-pity blocks the view of the tiny exit above.

Step in and look at the prisoners. Victims are chained to the walls. Victims of betrayal. Victims of abuse. Victims of the government, the system, the military, the world. They lift their chains as they lift their voices and wail. Loud and long they wail.

They grumble. They're angry at others who got what they didn't.

They sulk. The world is against them.

They accuse. The pictures of their enemies are darted to the wall.

They boast. "I followed the rules. I played fairly . . . in fact, better than anybody else."

They whine. "Nobody listens to me. Nobody remembers me. Nobody cares about me."

Angry. Sullen. Accusatory. Arrogant. Whiny. Put them all together in one word and spell it b-i-t-t-e-r. If you put them all in one person, that person is in the pit—the dungeon of bitterness.

The dungeon, deep and dark, is beckoning you to enter.

You can, you know. You've experienced enough hurt. You've been betrayed enough times. You have a history of rejections, don't you? Haven't you been left out, left behind, or left out in the cold? You are a candidate for the dungeon.

You can choose, like many, to chain yourself to your hurt.

Or you can choose, like some, to put away your hurts before they become hates. You can choose to go to the party. You have a place there. Your name is beside a plate. If you are a child of God, no one can take away your sonship.

Which is precisely what the father said to the older son. "Son, you are always with me, and all that I have is yours" (v. 31).

And that is precisely what the Father says to you. How does God deal with your bitter heart? He reminds you that what you have is more important than what you don't have. You still have your relationship with God. No one can take that. No one can touch it.

Your health can be taken and your money stolen—but your place at God's table is permanent.

The brother was bitter because he focused on what he didn't have and forgot what he did have. His father reminded him—and us—that he had everything he'd always had. He had his job. His place. His name. His inheritance. The only thing he didn't have was the spotlight. And because he wasn't content to share it—he missed the party.

It takes courage to set aside jealousy and rejoice with the

achievements of a rival. Would you like an example of someone who did?

Standing before ten thousand eyes is Abraham Lincoln. An uncomfortable Abraham Lincoln. His discomfort comes not from the thought of delivering his first inaugural address but from the ambitious efforts of well-meaning tailors. He's unaccustomed to such attire—formal black dress coat, silk vest, black trousers, and a glossy top hat. He holds a huge ebony cane with a golden head the size of an egg.

He approaches the platform with hat in one hand and cane in the other. He doesn't know what to do with either one. In the nervous silence that comes after the applause and before the speech, he searches for a spot to place them. He finally leans the cane in a corner of the railing, but he still doesn't know what to do with the hat. He could lay it on the podium, but it would take up too much room. Perhaps the floor . . . no, too dirty.

Just then, and not a moment too soon, a man steps forward and takes the hat, returns to his seat, and listens intently to Lincoln's speech.

Who is he? Lincoln's dearest friend. The president said of him, "He and I are about the best friends in the world."

He was one of the strongest supporters of the early stages of Lincoln's presidency. He was given the honor of escorting Mrs. Lincoln in the inaugural grand ball. As the storm of the Civil War began to boil, many of Lincoln's friends left, but not this one. He amplified his loyalty by touring the South as Lincoln's peace ambassador. He begged Southerners not to secede and Northerners to rally behind the president.

His efforts were great, but the wave of anger was greater. The country did divide, and civil war bloodied the nation. Lincoln's friend never lived to see it. He died three months after Lincoln's inauguration. Wearied by his travels, he succumbed to a fever, and Lincoln was left to face the war alone.

Upon hearing the news of his friend's death, Lincoln wept openly and ordered the White House flag to be flown at half-staff. Some feel Lincoln's friend would have been chosen as his running mate in 1864 and would thus have become president following the assassination of the Great Emancipator.

No one will ever know about that. But we do know that Lincoln had one true friend. And we can only imagine the number of times the memory of him brought warmth to a cold Oval Office. He was a model of friendship.

He was also a model of forgiveness.

This friend could just as easily have been an enemy. Long before he and Lincoln were allies, they were competitors—politicians pursuing the same office. And unfortunately, their debates are better known than their friendship. The debates between Abraham Lincoln and his dear friend, Stephen A. Douglas.

But on Lincoln's finest day, Douglas set aside their differences and held the hat of the president. Unlike the older brother, Douglas heard a higher call. And unlike the older brother, he was present at the party.

Wise are we if we do the same. Wise are we if we rise above our hurts. For if we do, we'll be present at the Father's final celebration. A party to end all parties. A party where no pouters will be permitted.

Why don't you come and join the fun?

4

WHEN YOU AND YOUR KIN CAN'T

Dealing with Difficult Relatives

> "My true brother and sister and
> mother are those who do what God
> wants."
>
> Mark 3:35

---

*G*ive me a word picture to describe a relative in your life who really bugs you."

I was asking the question of a half-dozen friends sitting around a lunch table. They all gave me one of those what-in-the-world? expressions. So I explained.

"I keep meeting people who can't deal with somebody in their family. Either their mother-in-law is a witch or their uncle is a bum or they have a father who treats them like they were never born."

Now their heads nodded. We were connecting. And the word pictures started coming.

"I've got a description," one volunteered. "A parasite on my neck. My wife has this brother who never works and always expects us to provide."

"A cactus wearing a silk shirt," said another. "It's my mother. She looks nice. Everyone thinks she's the greatest, but get close to her and she is prickly, dry, and . . . thirsty for life."

"A marble column," was the way another described an aunt. Dignified, noble, but high and hard.

"Tar baby in Brer Rabbit," someone responded. Everyone understood the reference except me. I didn't remember the story of Brer Rabbit. I asked for the short version. Wily Fox played a trick on Brer Rabbit. The fox made a doll out of tar and stuck it on the side of the road. When Rabbit saw the tar baby, he thought it was a person and stopped to visit.

It was a one-sided conversation. The tar baby's silence bothered the rabbit. He couldn't stand to be next to someone and not communicate with them. So in his frustration he hit the tar baby and stuck to it. He hit the tar baby again with the other hand and, you guessed it, the other hand got stuck.

"That's how we are with difficult relatives," my fable-using friend explained. "We're stuck to someone we can't communicate with."

Stuck is right. It's not as if they are a neighbor you can move away from or an employee you can fire. They are family. And you can choose your friends, but you can't . . . well, you know.

Odds are, you probably know very well.

You've probably got a tar baby in your life, someone you can't talk to and can't walk away from. A mother who whines, an uncle who slurps his soup, or a sister who flaunts her figure. A dad who is still waiting for you to get a real job or a mother-in-law who wonders why her daughter married you.

Tar-baby relationships—stuck together but falling apart.

It's like a crammed and jammed elevator. People thrust together by chance on a short journey, saying as little as possible. The only difference is you'll eventually get off the elevator and never see these folks again—not so with the difficult relative. Family reunions, Christmas, Thanksgiving, weddings, funerals— they'll be there.

And you'll be there sorting through the tough questions. Why does life get so *relatively* difficult? If we expect anyone to be sensitive to our needs, it is our family members. When we hurt physically, we want our family to respond. When we struggle emotionally, we want our family to know.

But sometimes they act like they don't know. Sometimes they act like they don't care.

In her book *Irregular People,* Joyce Landorf tells of a woman in her thirties who learned that she needed a mastectomy. She and her mother seldom communicated, so the daughter was apprehensive about telling her. One day over lunch, she decided to reveal the news. "Mother, I just learned that I am going to have a mastectomy."

The mother was silent. The daughter asked her if she had heard. The mother nodded her head. Then she calmly dismissed the subject by saying, "You know your sister has the best recipe for chicken enchiladas."

What can you do when those closest to you keep their distance? When you can get along with others, but you and your kin can't?

Does Jesus have anything to say about dealing with difficult relatives? Is there an example of Jesus bringing peace to a painful family? Yes, there is.

His own.

It may surprise you to know that Jesus had a difficult family. It may surprise you to know that Jesus had a family at all! You may not be aware that Jesus had brothers and sisters. He did. Quoting Jesus' hometown critics, Mark wrote, "[Jesus] is just the carpenter, the son of Mary and the brother of James, Joseph, Judas, and Simon. And his sisters are here with us" (Mark 6:3).

And it may surprise you to know that his family was less than perfect. They were. If your family doesn't appreciate you, take heart, neither did Jesus'. "A prophet is honored everywhere except in his hometown and with his own people and in his own home" (Mark 6:4).

I wonder what he meant when he said those last five words. He went to the synagogue where he was asked to speak. The people were proud that this hometown boy had done well—until they heard what he said. He referred to himself as the Messiah, the one to fulfill prophecy.

Their response? "Isn't this Joseph's son?" Translation? This is no Messiah! He's just like us! He's the plumber's kid from down the street. He's the accountant on the third floor. He's the construction worker who used to date my sister. God doesn't speak through familiar people.

One minute he was a hero, the next a heretic. Look what happens next. "They got up, forced Jesus out of town, and took him to the edge of the cliff on which the town was built. They planned to throw him off the edge, but Jesus walked through the crowd and went on his way" (Luke 4:29–30).

What an ugly moment! Jesus' neighborhood friends tried to kill him. But even uglier than what we see is what we don't see. Notice what is missing from this verse. Note what words should be there, but aren't. "They planned to throw him over the cliff, but Jesus' brothers came and stood up for him."

We'd like to read that, but we can't because it doesn't say that. That's not what happened. When Jesus was in trouble, his brothers were invisible.

They weren't always invisible, however. There was a time when they spoke. There was a time when they were seen with him in public. Not because they were proud of him but because they were ashamed of him. "His family . . . went to get him because they thought he was out of his mind" (Mark 3:21).

Jesus' siblings thought their brother was a lunatic. They weren't proud—they were embarrassed!

"He's off the deep end, Mom. You should hear what people are saying about him."

"People say he's loony."

"Yeah, somebody asked me why we don't do something about him."

"It's a good thing Dad isn't around to see what Jesus is doing."

Hurtful words spoken by those closest to Jesus.

Here are some more:

So Jesus' brothers said to him, "You should leave here and go to Judea so your followers there can see the miracles you do. Anyone who wants to be well known does not hide what he does. If you are doing these things, show yourself to the world." (Even Jesus' brothers did not believe in him.)

John 7:3–5

Listen to the sarcasm in those words! They drip with ridicule. How does Jesus put up with these guys? How can you believe in yourself when those who know you best don't? How can you move forward when your family wants to pull you back? When you and your family have two different agendas, what do you do?

Jesus gives us some answers.

It's worth noting that he didn't try to control his family's behavior, nor did he let their behavior control his. He didn't demand that they agree with him. He didn't sulk when they insulted him. He didn't make it his mission to try to please them.

Each of us has a fantasy that our family will be like the Waltons, an expectation that our dearest friends will be our next of kin. Jesus didn't have that expectation. Look how he defined his family: "My true brother and sister and mother are those who do what God wants" (Mark 3:35).

When Jesus' brothers didn't share his convictions, he didn't try to force them. He recognized that his spiritual family could provide what his physical family didn't. If Jesus himself couldn't force his family to share his convictions, what makes you think you can force yours?

We can't control the way our family responds to us. When it comes to the behavior of others toward us, our hands are tied. We have to move beyond the naive expectation that if we do good, people will treat us right. The fact is they may and they may not—we cannot control how people respond to us.

If your father is a jerk, you could be the world's best daughter and he still won't tell you so.

If your aunt doesn't like your career, you could change jobs a dozen times and still never satisfy her.

If your sister is always complaining about what you got and she didn't, you could give her everything and she still may not change.

As long as you think you can control people's behavior toward you, you are held in bondage by their opinions. If you think you can control their opinion and their opinion isn't positive, then guess who you have to blame? Yourself.

It's a game with unfair rules and fatal finishes. Jesus didn't play it, nor should you.

We don't know if Joseph affirmed his son Jesus in his ministry—but we know God did: "This is my Son, whom I love, and I am very pleased with him" (Matt. 3:17).

I can't assure you that your family will ever give you the blessing you seek, but I know God will. Let God give you what your family doesn't. If your earthly father doesn't affirm you, then let your heavenly Father take his place.

How do you do that? By emotionally accepting God as your father. You see, it's one thing to accept him as Lord, another to recognize him as Savior—but it's another matter entirely to accept him as Father.

To recognize God as Lord is to acknowledge that he is sovereign and supreme in the universe. To accept him as Savior is to accept his gift of salvation offered on the cross. To regard him as Father is to go a step further. Ideally, a father is the one in your life who provides and protects. That is exactly what God has done.

He has provided for your needs (Matt. 6:25–34). He has protected you from harm (Ps. 139:5). He has adopted you (Eph. 1:5). And he has given you his name (1 John 3:1).

God has proven himself as a faithful father. Now it falls to us to be trusting children. Let God give you what your family doesn't. Let him fill the void others have left. Rely upon him for your affirmation and encouragement. Look at Paul's words: "you are God's child, and *God will give you the blessing he promised,* because you are his child" (Gal. 4:7, emphasis added).

Having your family's approval is desirable but not necessary for happiness and not always possible. Jesus did not let the difficult dynamic of his family overshadow his call from God. And because he didn't, this chapter has a happy ending.

What happened to Jesus' family?

Mine with me a golden nugget hidden in a vein of the Book of Acts. "Then [the disciples] went back to Jerusalem from the Mount of Olives. . . . They all continued praying together with some women, *including Mary the mother of Jesus, and Jesus' brothers*" (Acts 1:12, 14, emphasis added).

What a change! The ones who mocked him now worship him. The ones who pitied him now pray for him. What if Jesus had disowned them? Or worse still, what if he'd suffocated his family with his demand for change?

He didn't. He instead gave them space, time, and grace. And because he did, they changed. How much did they change? One brother became an apostle (Gal. 1:19) and others became missionaries (1 Cor. 9:5).

So don't lose heart. God still changes families. A tar baby today might be your dearest friend tomorrow.

5

IT'S ALL RIGHT TO DREAM AGAIN

Facing Discouragement

At that time there was a strong earthquake. An angel of the Lord came down from heaven, went to the tomb, and rolled the stone away from the entrance. Then he sat on the stone. He was shining as bright as lightning, and his clothes were white as snow. The soldiers guarding the tomb shook with fear because of the angel, and they became like dead men.

The angel said to the women, "Don't be afraid. I know that you are looking for Jesus, who has been crucified. He is not here. He has risen from the dead as he said he would. Come and see the place where his body was. And go quickly and tell his followers, 'Jesus has risen from the dead. He is going into Galilee ahead of you, and you will see him there.'" Then the angel said, "Now I have told you."

The women left the tomb quickly. They were afraid, but they were also very happy. They ran to tell Jesus' followers what had happened. Suddenly, Jesus met them and said, "Greetings." The women came up to him, took hold of his feet, and worshiped him. Then Jesus said to them, "Don't be afraid. Go and tell my followers to go on to Galilee, and they will see me there."

Matthew 28:2–10

> "Don't be afraid. I know that you are
> looking for Jesus, who has been
> crucified. He is not here. He has risen
> from the dead as he said he would."
>
> Matthew 28:5

You know how you can read a story you think you know and then you read it again and see something you've never seen?

You know how you can read about the same event 100 times and then on the 101st hear something so striking and new that it makes you wonder if you slept through the other times?

Maybe it's because you started in the middle of the story instead of at the beginning. Or perhaps it's because someone else reads it aloud and pauses at a place where you normally wouldn't and POW! it hits you.

You grab the book and look at it, knowing that someone copied or read something wrong. But then you read it and well-how-do-you-do. Look at that!

Well, it happened to me. Today.

Only God knows how many times I've read the resurrection story. At least a couple of dozen Easters and a couple of hundred times in between. I've taught it. I've written about it. I've meditated on it. I've underlined it. But what I saw today I'd never seen before.

What did I see? Before I tell you, let me recount the story.

It's early dawn on Sunday morning and the sky is dark. Those, in fact, are John's words. "It was still dark . . ." (John 20:1).

It's a dark Sunday morning. It had been dark since Friday.

Dark with Peter's denial.

Dark with the disciples' betrayal.

Dark with Pilate's cowardice.

Dark with Christ's anguish.

Dark with Satan's glee.

The only ember of light is the small band of women standing at a distance from the cross—watching (Matt. 27:55).

Among them are two Marys, one the mother of James and Joseph and the other is Mary Magdalene. Why are they there? They are there to call his name. To be the final voices he hears before his death. To prepare his body for burial. They are there to clean the blood from his beard. To wipe the crimson from his legs. To close his eyes. To touch his face.

They are there. The last to leave Calvary and the first to arrive at the grave.

So early on that Sunday morning, they leave their pallets and walk out onto the tree-shadowed path. Theirs is a somber task. The morning promises only one encounter, an encounter with a corpse.

Remember, Mary and Mary don't know this is the first Easter. They are not hoping the tomb will be vacant. They aren't discussing what their response will be when they see Jesus. They have absolutely no idea that the grave has been vacated.

There was a time when they dared to dream such dreams. Not now. It's too late for the incredible. The feet that walked on water had been pierced. The hands that healed lepers had been stilled. Noble aspirations had been spiked into Friday's cross. Mary and Mary have come to place warm oils on a cold body and bid farewell to the one man who gave reason to their hopes.

But it isn't hope that leads the women up the mountain to the tomb. It is duty. Naked devotion. They expect nothing in return. What could Jesus give? What could a dead man offer? The two women are not climbing the mountain to receive, they are going to the tomb to give. Period.

There is no motivation more noble.

There are times when we, too, are called to love, expecting nothing in return. Times when we are called to give money to people who will never say thanks, to forgive those who won't forgive us, to come early and stay late when no one else notices.

Service prompted by duty. This is the call of discipleship.

Mary and Mary knew a task had to be done—Jesus' body had to be prepared for burial. Peter didn't offer to do it. Andrew didn't volunteer. The forgiven adulteress or healed lepers are nowhere to be seen. So the two Marys decide to do it.

I wonder if halfway to the tomb they had sat down and reconsidered. What if they'd looked at each other and shrugged, "What's the use?" What if they had given up? What if one had thrown up her arms in frustration and bemoaned, "I'm tired of being the only one who cares. Let Andrew do something for a change. Let Nathaniel show some leadership."

Whether or not they were tempted to, I'm glad they didn't quit. That would have been tragic. You see, we know something they didn't. We know the Father was watching. Mary and Mary thought they were alone. They weren't. They thought their journey was unnoticed. They were wrong. God knew. He was watching them walk up the mountain. He was measuring their steps. He was smiling at their hearts and thrilled at their devotion. And he had a surprise waiting for them.

> At that time there was a strong earthquake. An angel of the Lord came down from heaven, went to the tomb, and rolled the stone away from the entrance. Then he sat on the stone. He was shining bright as lightning, and his clothes were white as snow. The soldiers guarding the tomb shook with fear because of the angel, and they became like dead men.
>
> Matthew 28:2–4

(Now, read carefully, this is what I noticed for the first time today.)

Why did the angel move the stone? For whom did he roll away the rock?

For Jesus? That's what I always thought. I just assumed that the angel moved the stone so Jesus could come out. But think about it. Did the stone have to be removed in order for Jesus to exit? Did God have to have help? Was the death conqueror so weak that he couldn't push away a rock? ("Hey, could somebody out there move this rock so I can get out?")

I don't think so. The text gives the impression that Jesus was already out when the stone was moved! Nowhere do the Gospels say that the angel moved the stone for Jesus. For whom, then, was the stone moved?

Listen to what the angel says: "Come and see the place where his body was" (v. 6).

The stone was moved—not for Jesus—but for the women; not so Jesus could come out, but so the women could see in!

Mary looks at Mary and Mary is grinning the same grin she had when the bread and fish kept coming out of the basket. The old passion flares. Suddenly it's all right to dream again.

"Go quickly and tell his followers, 'Jesus has risen from the dead. He is going into Galilee ahead of you, and you will see him there'" (v. 7).

Mary and Mary don't have to be told twice. They turn and start running to Jerusalem. The darkness is gone. The sun is up. The Son is out. But the Son isn't finished.

One surprise still awaits them.

"Suddenly, Jesus met them and said, 'Greetings.' The women came up to him, took hold of his feet, and worshiped him. Then Jesus said to them, 'Don't be afraid. Go and tell my followers to go on to Galilee, and they will see me there'" (vv. 9–10).

The God of surprises strikes again. It's as if he said, "I can't wait any longer. They came this far to see me; I'm going to drop in on them."

God does that for the faithful. Just when the womb gets too old for babies, Sarai gets pregnant. Just when the failure is too great for grace, David is pardoned. And just when the road is too dark for Mary and Mary, the angel glows and the Savior shows and the two women will never be the same.

The lesson? Three words. Don't give up.

Is the trail dark? Don't sit.

Is the road long? Don't stop.

Is the night black? Don't quit.

God is watching. For all you know right at this moment he may be telling the angel to move the stone.

The check may be in the mail.

The apology may be in the making.

The job contract may be on the desk.

Don't quit. For if you do, you may miss the answer to your prayers.

God still sends angels. And God still moves stones.

6

SOUR MILK

Overcoming a Bad Attitude

While Jesus and his followers were traveling, Jesus went into a town. A woman named Martha let Jesus stay at her house. Martha had a sister named Mary, who was sitting at Jesus' feet and listening to him teach. But Martha was busy with all the work to be done. She went in and said, "Lord, don't you care that my sister has left me alone to do all the work? Tell her to help me."

But the Lord answered her, "Martha, Martha, you are worried and upset about many things. Only one thing is important. Mary has chosen the better thing, and it will never be taken away from her."

Luke 10:38–42

> Do everything without complaining or
> arguing. Then you will be innocent
> and without any wrong.
>
> Philippians 2:14–15

I love milk. I am a confessed milkaholic. One of the saddest days of my life was when I learned that whole milk was unhealthy. With great reluctance I have adapted to the watered-down version—but on occasion I still allow myself the hallowed ecstasy of a cold glass of whole milk and a hot, gooey, chocolate-chip cookie.

In my years of appreciating the fine fruit of the cow I have learned that a high price is paid for leaving milk out of the refrigerator. (On one occasion I spewed the spoiled stuff all over the kitchen cabinet.) Sweet milk turns sour from being too warm too long.

Sweet dispositions turn sour for the same reason. Let aggravation stew without a period of cooling down, and the result? A bad, bitter, clabberish attitude.

The tenth chapter of Luke describes the step-by-step process of the sweet becoming sour.

It's the story of Martha. A dear soul given to hospitality and organization. More frugal than frivolous, more practical than pensive, her household is a tight ship and she is a stern captain. Ask her to choose between a book and a broom, and she'll take the broom.

Mary, however, will take the book. Mary is Martha's sister. Same parents, different priorities. Martha has things to do. Mary has thoughts to think. The dishes can wait. Let Martha go to the market; Mary will go to the library.

Two sisters. Two personalities. And as long as they understand each other, it's hand in glove. But when the one resents the other, it's flint and stone.

Let's say we quietly step in the back door of Martha's kitchen and I'll show you what I mean. (One warning: Stay away from the milk; it's beginning to sour.)

Shhh, there she is. Over by the table. The one wearing the apron. My, look at her work! I told you this lady knows how to run a kitchen. How does she do that? Stirring with one hand, cracking eggs with the other. And nothing spills. She knows what she's doing.

Must be a big crowd. There's lots of food. That's them laughing in the next room. Sounds like they're having fun.

But Martha isn't. One look at the flour-covered scowl will tell you that.

"Stupid sister."

What? Did you hear her mumble something?

"That Mary. Here I am alone in the kitchen while she's out there."

Hmm. Seems the oven isn't the only thing hot in here.

"Wouldn't have invited Jesus over if I'd known he was gonna bring the whole army. Those guys eat like horses, and that Peter always belches."

Oh boy. She's miffed. Look at her glaring over her shoulder through the doorway. That's Mary she's staring at. The one seated on the floor, listening to Jesus.

"Little sweet sister . . . always ready to listen and never ready to work. I wouldn't mind sitting down myself. But all I do is cook and sew, cook and sew. Well, enough is enough!"

Watch out! There she goes. Someone's about to get it.

"Lord, don't you care that my sister has left me alone to do all the work? Tell her to help me" (v. 40).

Suddenly the room goes silent, deathly silent except for the tap-tap-tapping of Martha's foot on the stone floor and the slapping of a wooden spoon in her palm. She looms above the others—flour on her cheeks and fire in her eyes.

We have to chuckle at the expression on the faces of the disciples. They stare wide-eyed at this fury that hell hath not known. And poor Mary, flushed red with embarrassment, sighs and sinks lower to the floor.

Only Jesus speaks. For only Jesus understands the problem. The problem is not the large crowd. The problem is not Mary's choice to listen. The problem is not Martha's choice to host. The problem is Martha's heart, a heart soured with anxiety.

"Martha, Martha, you are worried and upset about many things" (v. 41). Bless her heart, Martha wanted to do right. But bless her heart, her heart was wrong. Her heart, Jesus said, was worried. As a result she turned from a happy servant into a beast of burden. She was worried: worried about cooking, worried about pleasing, worried about too much.

I like what my favorite theologian Erma Bombeck has to say about worrying:

> I've always worried a lot and frankly, I'm good at it. I worry about introducing people and going blank when I get to my mother. I worry about a shortage of ball bearings; a snake coming up through the kitchen drain. I worry about the world ending at midnight and getting stuck with three hours on a twenty-four hour cold capsule. I worry about getting into the *Guinness World Book of Records* under "Pregnancy: Oldest Recorded Birth." I worry what the dog thinks when he sees me coming out of the shower; that one of my children will marry an Eskimo who will set me adrift on an iceberg when I can no longer feed myself. I worry about salesladies following me into the fitting room, oil slicks, and Carol Channing going bald. I worry about scientists discovering someday that lettuce has been fattening all along.

Apparently Martha worried too much, too. So much so that she started bossing God around. Worry will do that to you. It makes you forget who's in charge.

What makes this case interesting, however, is that Martha is worried about something good. She's having Jesus over for dinner. She's literally serving God. Her aim was to please Jesus. But she made a common, yet dangerous mistake. As she began to work for him, her work became more important than her Lord. What began as a way to serve Jesus, slowly and subtly became a way to serve self.

Maybe the process went something like this. As she began to prepare the meal, she anticipated the compliments on the food. As she set the table, she imagined the approval. She could just picture it. Jesus would enter the house and thank her for all her work. He would tell the disciples to give her a standing ovation. John would cite her as an example of hospitality and dedicate a chapter in the Bible to her.

Then women would come from miles around to ask her how she learned to be such a kind and humble servant. The rest of her days would be spent directing a school of servanthood—with Jesus as the director and Martha as the professor.

But things didn't turn out like she'd planned. She didn't get the attention she sought. No standing ovation. No compliments. No adulations. No school. No one noticed. And that irritated her. Martha is long on anxiety and short on memory. She has forgotten that the invitation was her idea. She has forgotten that Mary has every right to be with Jesus. And most of all, she has forgotten that the meal is to honor Jesus, not Martha.

I know exactly how Martha feels. For I've been in Martha's kitchen. Or better, I've been in Max's office.

I know what it's like to set out to serve God and end up serving self. I've labored long and hard over sermons only to have my feelings hurt if they aren't complimented. I've pushed myself deeply into a manuscript only to catch myself daydreaming about the postpublication compliments. I've spoken to conference audiences about the sufferings of Christ and then gotten frustrated that the hotel room wasn't ready.

It's easy to forget who is the servant and who is to be served.

Satan knows that. This tool of distortion is one of Satan's slyest. Note: He didn't take Martha out of the kitchen; he took away her purpose in the kitchen. The adversary won't turn you against the church; he will turn you toward yourself in the church. He won't take you away from your ministry; he'll disillusion you in your ministry.

And when the focus is on yourself, you do what Martha did—you worry. You become anxious about many things. You worry that:

> Your co-workers won't appreciate you.
> Your leaders will overwork you.
> Your superintendent won't understand you.
> Your congregation won't support you.

With time, your agenda becomes more important than God's. You're more concerned with presenting self than pleasing him. And you may even find yourself doubting God's judgment.

"Lord, don't you care that my sister has left me alone to do all the work? Tell her to help me" (v. 40).

Don't you know Martha regretted saying that! I bet that after she cooled down, she would have loved to have those words back. I imagine she wished she'd heeded Solomon's counsel: "A rebel shouts in anger . . . a wise man holds his temper in and cools it" (Prov. 29:11 TLB).

There is a principle here. To keep an attitude from souring, treat it like you would a cup of milk. Cool it off.

Martha's life was cluttered. She needed a break. "Martha, Martha, you are worried and upset about many things," the Master explained to her. "Only one thing is important. Mary has chosen [it]" (v. 41–42).

What had Mary chosen? She had chosen to sit at the feet of Christ. God is more pleased with the quiet attention of a sincere servant than the noisy service of a sour one.

By the way, this story could easily have been reversed. Mary could have been the one to get angry. The sister on the floor could have resented the sister at the sink. Mary could have grabbed Jesus and dragged him into the kitchen and said, "Tell Martha to quit being so productive and to get reflective. Why do I have to do all the thinking and praying around here?"

What matters more than the type of service is the heart behind the service. A bad attitude spoils the gift we leave on the altar for God.

Maybe you've heard the joke about the fellow who prayed with a bad attitude?

"Why," he asked, "has my brother been blessed with wealth and I with nothing? All of my life I have never missed a single day without saying morning and evening prayers. My church attendance has been perfect. I have always loved my neighbor and given my money. Yet now, as I near the end of my life, I can hardly afford to pay my rent.

"My brother, on the other hand, drinks and gambles and plays all the time. Yet he has more money than he can count. I don't ask you to punish him, but tell me, why has he been given so much and I have been given nothing?"

"Because," God replied, "you're such a self-righteous pain in the neck."

Guard your attitude.

God has gifted you with talents. He has done the same to your neighbor. If you concern yourself with your neighbor's talents, you will neglect yours. But if you concern yourself with yours, you could inspire both.

7

A Crazy Hunch and a High Hope

Genuine Gestures of Faith

So Jesus went with him.

A large crowd followed Jesus and pushed very close around him. Among them was a woman who had been bleeding for twelve years. She had suffered very much from many doctors and had spent all the money she had, but instead of improving, she was getting worse. When the woman heard about Jesus, she came up behind him in the crowd and touched his coat. She thought, "If I can just touch his clothes, I will be healed." Instantly her bleeding stopped, and she felt in her body that she was healed from her disease.

At once Jesus felt power go out from him. So he turned around in the crowd and asked, "Who touched my clothes?"

His followers said, "Look at how many people are pushing against you! And you ask, 'Who touched me?'"

But Jesus continued looking around to see who had touched him. The woman, knowing that she was healed, came and fell at Jesus' feet. Shaking with fear, she told him the whole truth. Jesus said to her, "Dear woman, you are made well because you believed. Go in peace; be healed of your disease."

Mark 5:24–34

$\mathcal{A}$ clock for Christmas is not the kind of gift that thrills an eight-
year-old boy, but I said thank you and took it to my bedroom,
put it on the nightstand, and plugged it in.

It was a square-faced Bulova. It didn't have moving num-
bers—it had rotating hands. It didn't play tapes or CDs, but over
the years it developed a slight, soothing hum that could be heard
when the room was quiet.

Today you can buy clocks that sound like rain when it's
time to sleep and like your mother when it's time to wake up.
But not this one. Its alarm could make the dogs howl. Forget
snooze buttons. Just pick it up and chunk it across the room.
It was a Neanderthal model. It wouldn't net fifty cents at a garage sale in this day of digital clocks and musical alarms.

But still, over time, I grew attached to it. People don't usually get sentimental about electric clocks, but I did about this
one. Not because of its accuracy, it was always a bit slow. Nor
the hum, which I didn't mind. I liked it because of the light.

You see, this clock glowed in the dark.

All day, every day it soaked up the light. It sponged up the
sun. The hands were little sticks of ticks and time and sunshine.
And when the night came, the clock was ready. When I flicked
off the light to sleep, the little clock flicked on its light and

shined. Not much light, but when your world is dark, just a little seems like a lot.

Somewhat like the light a woman got when she met Jesus.

We don't know her name, but we know her situation. Her world was midnight black. Grope-in-the-dark-and-hope-for-help black. Read these two verses and see what I mean:

> A large crowd followed Jesus and pushed very close around him. Among them was a woman who had been bleeding for twelve years. She had suffered very much from many doctors and had spent all the money she had, but instead of improving, she was getting worse.
>
> Mark 5:24–26

She was a bruised reed: "bleeding for twelve years," "suffered very much," "spent all the money she had," and "getting worse."

A chronic menstrual disorder. A perpetual issue of blood. Such a condition would be difficult for any woman of any era. But for a Jewess, nothing could be worse. No part of her life was left unaffected.

Sexually . . . she could not touch her husband.

Maternally . . . she could not bear children.

Domestically . . . anything she touched was considered unclean. No washing dishes. No sweeping floors.

Spiritually . . . she was not allowed to enter the temple.

She was physically exhausted and socially ostracized.

She had sought help "under the care of many doctors" (v. 26 NIV). The Talmud gives no fewer than eleven cures for such a condition. No doubt she had tried them all. Some were legitimate treatments. Others, such as carrying the ashes of an ostrich egg in a linen cloth, were hollow superstitions.

She "had spent all she had" (v. 26 NIV). To dump financial strain on top of the physical strain is to add insult to injury. A friend battling cancer told me that the hounding of the creditors who demand payments for ongoing medical treatment is just as devastating as the pain.

"Instead of getting better she grew worse" (v. 26 NIV). She was a bruised reed. She awoke daily in a body that no one wanted. She is down to her last prayer. And on the day we encounter her, she's about to pray it.

By the time she gets to Jesus, he is surrounded by people. He's on his way to help the daughter of Jairus, the most important man in the community. What are the odds that he will interrupt an urgent mission with a high official to help the likes of her? Very few. But what are the odds that she will survive if she doesn't take a chance? Fewer still. So she takes a chance.

"If I can just touch his clothes," she thinks, "I will be healed" (v. 28).

Risky decision. To touch him, she will have to touch the people. If one of them recognizes her . . . hello rebuke, good-bye cure. But what choice does she have? She has no money, no clout, no friends, no solutions. All she has is a crazy hunch that Jesus can help and a high hope that he will.

Maybe that's all you have: a crazy hunch and a high hope. You have nothing to give. But you are hurting. And all you have to offer him is your hurt.

Maybe that has kept you from coming to God. Oh, you've taken a step or two in his direction. But then you saw the other people around him. They seemed so clean, so neat, so trim and fit in their faith. And when you saw them, they blocked your view of him. So you stepped back.

If that describes you, note carefully, only one person was commended that day for having faith. It wasn't a wealthy giver. It wasn't a loyal follower. It wasn't an acclaimed teacher. It was a shame-struck, penniless outcast who clutched onto her hunch that he could and her hope that he would.

Which, by the way, isn't a bad definition of faith: *A conviction that he can and a hope that he will*. Sounds similar to the definition of faith given by the Bible. "Without faith no one can please God. Anyone who comes to God must believe that he is real and that he rewards those who truly want to find him" (Heb. 11:6).

Not too complicated is it? Faith is the belief that God is real and that God is good. Faith is not a mystical experience or a midnight vision or a voice in the forest . . . it is a choice to believe that the one who made it all hasn't left it all and that he still sends light into shadows and responds to gestures of faith.

There was no guarantee, of course. She hoped he'd respond . . . she longed for it . . . but she didn't know if he would. All she knew was that he was there and that he was good. That's faith.

Faith is not the belief that God will do what you want. Faith is the belief that God will do what is right.

"Blessed are the dirt-poor, nothing-to-give, trapped-in-a-corner, destitute, diseased," Jesus said, "for theirs is the kingdom of heaven" (Matt. 5:6, my translation).

God's economy is upside down (or rightside up and ours is upside down!). God says that the more hopeless your circumstance, the more likely your salvation. The greater your cares, the more genuine your prayers. The darker the room, the greater the need for light.

Which takes us back to my clock. When it was daylight, I never appreciated my little Bulova's capacity to glow in the dark. But as the shadows grew, so did my gratitude.

A healthy lady never would have appreciated the power of a touch of the hem of his robe. But this woman was sick . . . and when her dilemma met his dedication, a miracle occurred.

Her part in the healing was very small. All she did was extend her arm through the crowd.

"If only I can touch him."

What's important is not the form of the effort but the fact of the effort. The fact is, she did something. She refused to settle for sickness another day and resolved to make a move.

Healing begins when we do something. Healing begins when we reach out. Healing starts when we take a step.

God's help is near and always available, but it is only given to those who seek it. Nothing results from apathy. The great work in this story is the mighty healing that occurred. But the great truth is that the healing began with her touch. And with that small, courageous gesture, she experienced Jesus' tender power.

Compared to God's part, our part is minuscule but necessary. We don't have to do much, *but we do have to do something*.

Write a letter.

Ask forgiveness.

Call a counselor.

Confess.

Call Mom.

Visit a doctor.

Be baptized.

Feed a hungry person.

Pray.

Teach.

Go.

Do something that demonstrates faith. For faith with no effort is no faith at all. *God will respond*. He has never rejected a genuine gesture of faith. Never.

God honors radical, risk-taking faith.

When arks are built, lives are saved. When soldiers march, Jerichos tumble. When staffs are raised, seas still open. When a lunch is shared, thousands are fed. And when a garment is touched—whether by the hand of an anemic woman in Galilee or by the prayers of a beggar in Bangladesh—Jesus stops. He stops and responds.

Mark can tell you. When this woman touched Christ, two things happened that happen nowhere else in the Bible. He recorded them both.

First, Jesus heals before he knows it. The power left automatically and instantaneously. It's as if the Father short-circuited the system and the divinity of Christ was a step ahead of the humanity of Christ.

Her need summoned his help. No neon lights or loud shouts. No razzle-dazzle. No fanfare. No hoopla. No splash. Just help.

Just like my dark room brought the light out of my clock, our dark world brings out the light of God.

Second, he calls her *daughter*. "Daughter, your faith has made you well" (v. 34 NKJV) It's the only time Jesus calls *any* woman *anywhere* daughter. Imagine how that made her feel! Who could remember the last time she received a term of affection? Who knew the last time kind eyes had met hers?

Leo Tolstoy, the great Russian writer, tells of the time he was walking down the street and passed a beggar. Tolstoy reached into his pocket to give the beggar some money, but his pocket was empty. Tolstoy turned to the man and said, "I'm sorry, my brother, but I have nothing to give."

The beggar brightened and said, "You have given me more than I asked for—you have called me brother."

To the loved, a word of affection is a morsel, but to the love-starved, a word of affection can be a feast.

And Jesus gave this woman a banquet.

Tradition holds that she never forgot what Jesus did. Legend states that she stayed with Jesus and followed him as he carried his cross up Calvary. Some believe she was Veronica, the woman who walked the road to the cross with him. And when the sweat and blood were stinging his eyes, she wiped his forehead.

She, at an hour of great need, received his touch—and he, at an hour of pain, received hers. We don't know if the legend is true, but we know it could be. And I don't know if the same has happened to you, but I know it can.

8

FOREVER YOUNG

How to Love Growing Old

> "Whoever tries to keep his life safe will
> lose it, and the man who is prepared to
> lose his life will preserve it."
>
> Luke 17:33 PHILLIPS

---

*D*on't you hate it when someone else reminds you?

The barber: "Getting a little thin on top here, Joe."

The stylist: "Next time you come in, Sue, we'll do something about these gray streaks."

The invitation: "You are invited to your thirtieth high school reunion."

Your kids: "Tell me again, who were the Rolling Stones?"

Your doctor: "Nothing to worry about, Bill. Your condition is common for folks in their mid-age."

The dawning of old age. The first pages of the final chapters. A golden speck appears on the green leaves of your life, and you are brought face to wrinkled face with the fact that you are getting older.

And though we joke ("Old age is when you sink your teeth into a steak . . . and they stay there"), not everyone laughs. Especially one who has been taught to treasure youth.

And weren't we all?

For decades you worried about everything except getting old. Out of all the things you couldn't count on, there was one thing you could, and that was your youth. You could eat like a horse and not look like one. All the schoolteachers were older than you. Professional athletes were about the same age as your older brother. Life was an open highway, and death was a millennium away.

But then they came, the subtle messages of mortality:

> You buy your first life insurance policy and it includes burial and funeral expenses.
>
> Your carpool friends ask you why you squint when you read road signs.
>
> The kid carrying your groceries calls you "Ma'am."

At first it's just raindrop reminders splashing on your water-color convictions of perpetual youth. With time, however, the raindrops become steady and stronger.

Everything hurts when you wake up. What doesn't hurt, doesn't work.

Your parents begin acting like your children.

The smile lines don't go away when you stop smiling.

And then—boom! The rain becomes a torrent. The gentle taps become thunder. Cardiac arrest. Empty nest. Forty candles. Bifocals. Boom. Boom! BOOM!

Now there is no denial. Ponce de Leon didn't find the fountain of youth, and neither will you. Oh, but how we try. Barbells get pumped. Black hair gone gray goes black again, or better yet, blond. The van is traded in on a truck, a four-wheel-drive monster that will tackle the treacherous ravines of the interstate. The face gets stretched. The chin gets tucked. Breasts get a lift.

But try as we might, the calendar pages still turn. The clocks still tick. And the body still grows older. And with every new pill we take we are reminded that growing old is a pill that has to be swallowed.

But why does the pill go down so slowly? Why is it so hard to accept? What is it about birthdays that causes us to quiver so?

Certainly part of the problem is the mirror (or at least the reflection in it). What was tight now sags. What once swung now bounces. Time, as they say, is a great healer, but it's a lousy beautician.

Or, for others, there is failure. What you set out to do, you didn't. You set out to avoid the trap of suburbia; now you're making mortgage payments. You swore you'd never be a corporate puppet, but now your closet is full of gray flannels. You determined to leave a legacy, but all you've left so far is a trail of diapers and check stubs.

But the real pain is deeper. For some it is the hollowness of success. Life at the top of the ladder can be lonely. Mahogany desks grow cold. Sales awards tarnish. Diplomas fade. Sometimes a dream-come-true world has come true and it's less than you'd hoped.

Regret becomes a major pastime. The plumber wishes he'd gone to medical school and the doctor wishes he were a plumber. The woman who works regrets the time she didn't spend with her kids and the stay-at-home mom wishes she had a career.

It can get even worse. Regret can lead to rebellion. Rebellion against the demands. Rebellion against the mundane. Rebellion against the ho-hum. Rebellion against whatever ties you down: your job, your government, your station wagon, or worse still . . . your family.

Those who rebel—those who choose to roam the back alleys of escape—are prime candidates to stumble into one of Satan's oldest pits . . . adultery.

A pretty, young secretary from down the hall brings some papers as well as some sympathy into your office . . .

The man next door says he can't believe you've had four kids and kept your figure so trim . . .

The David in us calls for Bathsheba. Potiphar's wife looks at Joseph. A romp is taken in the greener grass and the hurt begins.

Let me be very clear with my point: Growing old can be dangerous. The trail is treacherous and the pitfalls are many. One is wise to be prepared. You know it's coming. It's not like God kept the process a secret. It's not like you are blazing a trail as you grow older. It's not as if no one has ever done it before. Look around you. You have ample opportunity to prepare and ample case studies to consider. If growing old catches you by surprise, don't blame God. He gave you plenty of warning. He also gave you plenty of advice.

Want some examples? Glad you asked. How about Luke 17:33?

"Whoever tries to keep his life safe will lose it, and the man who is prepared to lose his life will preserve it" (PHILLIPS).

"There are two ways to view life," Jesus is saying, "those who protect it or those who pursue it. The wisest are not the ones with the most years in their lives, but the most life in their years."

What Annie Dillard says about writing in *The Writing Life* is true about life: "One of the few things I know about writing is this: spend it all, play it, lose it all, right away, every time. Do not hoard what seems good for a later place in the book, or for another book; give it, give it all, give it now."

There is a rawness and a wonder to life. Pursue it. Hunt for it. Sell out to get it. Don't listen to the whines of those who have settled for a second-rate life and want you to do the same so they won't feel guilty. Your goal is not to live long; it's to live.

Jesus says the options are clear. On one side there is the voice of safety. You can build a fire in the hearth, stay inside, and stay warm and dry and safe. You can't get hurt if you never get out, right? You can't be criticized for what you don't try, right? You can't fall if you don't take a stand, right? You can't lose your balance if you never climb, right? So, don't try it. Take the safe route.

Or you can hear the voice of adventure—God's adventure. Instead of building a fire in your hearth, build a fire in your heart. Follow God's impulses. Adopt the child. Move overseas. Teach the class. Change careers. Run for office. Make a difference. Sure it isn't safe, but what is?

You think staying inside out of the cold is safe? Jesus disagrees. "Whoever tries to keep his life safe will lose it." I like the words of General Douglas MacArthur when he was seventy-eight: "Nobody grows old by merely living a number of years.

People grow old by deserting their ideals. Years may wrinkle the skin, but to give up interest wrinkles the soul."

Charles Lindbergh, the first pilot to fly across the Atlantic, had this to say about living safely:

> I decided that if I could fly for ten years before I was killed in a crash, it would be a worthwhile trade for an ordinary lifetime. . . . Who valued life more highly, the aviators who spent it on the art they loved, or the misers who doled it out like pennies through their antlike days?

Once again, read Jesus' admonition. "Whoever tries to keep his life safe will lose it, and the man who is prepared to lose his life will preserve it."

Reclaim the curiosity of your childhood. Just because you're near the top of the hill doesn't mean you've passed your peak.

Your last chapters can be your best. Your final song can be your greatest. It could be that all of your life has prepared you for a grand exit. God's oldest have always been among his choicest.

It was his octogenarian activities that got Moses into your Bible. Old and mellow Abraham was much wiser than young and brash Abram. Caleb still claimed his mountain when he was eighty-five. Anna was an eighty-five-year-old widow who had enough strength to pray for the Messiah and enough vision to recognize him when he came.

And look at John, the aged apostle John. The last of the apostles. The dear friend of Jesus. Surely his final years will be quiet and restful. Surely John has done what he came to do.

Nope. Don't tell that to John. And don't tell that to God. For neither of them was finished. John had one more chapter to write. What was intended to be an island of isolation became a place of inspiration, and in his final years John wrote the final book of the Bible. Could it be that all of John's life had led to this moment?

Such is the ring of Robert Browning's well-known words:

Grow old along with me
The best is yet to be
The last of life,
For which the first was made.

The final years can be your best. Ask Othmar Ammann. During his "retirement" he designed such structures as the Connecticut and New Jersey turnpikes, the Pittsburgh Civic Arena, Dulles Airport, the Throngs Neck Bridge, and the Verrazano Narrows Bridge.

Heinrich Schliemann would agree. He retired from business to look for Homer's legendary city of Troy. He found it.

Winston Churchill was worthy of taking a rest after World War II, but he didn't take it. Instead he took up a pen and won the Nobel Prize in literature at the age of seventy-nine.

Some get old and go fishing. Others get old and go hunting—they go hunting for what they always wanted to do. And they do it.

A friend of the late American jurist Oliver Wendell Holmes asked him why he had taken up the study of Greek at the age of ninety-four. Holmes replied, "Well, my good sir, it's now or never."

When J. C. Penney was ninety-five years old, he affirmed, "My eyesight may be getting weaker, but my vision is increasing."

As we get older, our vision should improve. Not our vision of earth but our vision of heaven. Those who have spent their life looking for heaven gain a skip in their step as the city comes into view. After Michelangelo died, someone found in his studio a piece of paper on which he had written a note to his apprentice. In the handwriting of his old age the great artist wrote: "Draw, Antonio, draw, and do not waste time."

Well-founded urgency, Michelangelo. Time slips. Days pass. Years fade. And life ends. And what we came to do must be done while there is time.

We would think it bizarre for a traveler not to be prepared for the end of the journey. We would pity the poor passenger who never read his itinerary. We'd be bewildered by someone who thought the purpose of the trip was the trip.

And for that person some of the saddest words in Scripture were penned. "The harvest is past, / The summer is ended, / And we are not saved" (Jer. 8:20 NKJV).

Others, however, are anticipating the destination. I hope you are. And I hope you'll be ready when you get home. For you, age is no enemy. Age is a mile-marker—a gentle reminder that home has never been so near.

Tell that to your barber.

9

READ THE STORY

When Others Let You Down

That same day two of Jesus' followers were going to a town named Emmaus, about seven miles from Jerusalem. They were talking about everything that had happened. While they were talking and discussing, Jesus himself came near and began walking with them, but they were kept from recognizing him. Then he said, "What are these things you are talking about while you walk?"

The two followers stopped, looking very sad. The one named Cleopas answered, "Are you the only visitor in Jerusalem who does not know what just happened there?"

Jesus said to them, "What are you talking about?"

They said, "About Jesus of Nazareth. He was a prophet who said and did many powerful things before God and all the people. Our leaders and the leading priests handed him over to be sentenced to death, and they crucified him. But we were hoping that he would free Israel. Besides this, it is now the third day since this happened. And today some women among us amazed us. Early this morning they went to the tomb, but they did not find his body there. They came and told us that they had seen a vision of angels who said that Jesus was alive! So some of our group went to the tomb, too. They found it just as the women said, but they did not see Jesus."

Then Jesus said to them, "You are foolish and slow to believe everything the prophets said. They said that the Christ must suffer these things before he enters his glory." Then starting with what Moses and all the prophets had said about him, Jesus began to explain everything that had been written about himself in the Scriptures.

They came near the town of Emmaus, and Jesus acted as if he were going farther. But they begged him, "Stay with us, because it is late; it is almost night." So he went in to stay with them.

When Jesus was at the table with them, he took some bread, gave thanks, divided it, and gave it to them. And then, they *were allowed to recognize Jesus. But when they saw who he was, he disappeared. They said to each other, "It felt like a fire burning in us when Jesus talked to us on the road and explained the Scriptures to us."*

So the two followers got up at once and went back to Jerusalem. There they found the eleven apostles and others gathered. They were saying, "The Lord really has risen from the dead! He showed himself to Simon."

Then the two followers told what had happened on the road and how they recognized Jesus when he divided the bread.

Luke 24:13–35

> They said to each other, "It felt like a
> fire burning in us when Jesus talked
> to us on the road and explained the
> Scriptures to us."
>
> Luke 24:32

---

*T*en-year-old Phineas was up before the sun was. He'd scarcely slept the night before. And long before a sound was heard in the house, he was downstairs with his bag packed, ready to climb into the wagon.

The year was 1820. And Phineas was about to see an island. His island. The island promised to him at birth. The day he was born, his grandfather presented newborn Phineas with a deed, a sizable portion of Connecticut land called Ivy Island. And to-day, for the first time, Phineas was to see it.

Not every boy is born a proprietor. Phineas's parents were always quick to remind their son of this. They urged him not to forget them when he came of age. Neighbors feared that the young landowner wouldn't want to play with their children.

Their concerns were legitimate. Phineas was different from his playmates. While they dreamed of dragons and knights, his fantasies were of Ivy Island. Someday he would be lord of his own territory. He'd build a house. Start a farm. Raise cattle. Rule his domain.

When you own an island you feel important.

When you own an island, you want to see it. Phineas had yet to see his. He pleaded with his father to take him to the is-land and, finally, in the summer of 1820, his father agreed.

Three sleepless nights preceded the expedition. Then, early that morning, Phineas, his father, and a hired hand climbed into the buggy and began the long-anticipated journey. Finally, Phineas would see his land.

He could scarcely sit still. At the top of each hill he would ask, "Are we nearly there? Can I see it from here?" And his father would encourage him to be patient and assure him that they were drawing near.

Finally, his dad pointed north beyond a meadow to a row of tall trees stretching into the sky.

"There," he said. "There is Ivy Island."

Phineas was overcome. He jumped from the wagon and dashed through the meadow, leaving his father far behind. He raced to the row of trees into an opening from which Ivy Island was visible.

When he saw the land he stopped. His heart sank.

Ivy Island was five acres of snake-infested marshland. His grandfather had called it the most valuable land in Connecticut. But it was worthless. His father had told him it was a generous gift. It wasn't. It was a joke . . . a cruel joke. As stunned Phineas stared, the father and the hired hand roared with laughter.

Phineas was not the fortunate beneficiary of the family. He was the laughingstock of the family. Grandfather Taylor had played a joke on his heir.

Phineas didn't laugh. Nor did he forget. That disappointment shaped his life. He, the deceived, made a lifestyle out of deception. The little boy fooled made a career out of fooling people.

He even may have fooled you.

You don't know him as Phineas. You know him as P.T. You don't know him as a landowner; you know him as a promoter. You know him as the one who coined the phrase, "There's a sucker born every minute." He spent his life proving it. Such was the life of P.T.—P. T. Barnum.

And such is the life of many others, many others who have been told they'd be taken to the Promised Land only to find themselves taken to the swamp.

I shared a ride to the airport this week with a businessman who a decade ago had an income twenty times what he has today. That was before his industry slumped. That was before he went broke.

After last Sunday's sermon a woman from another town asked what to do with her memories. I asked her what she meant. "I want to go to church, but I was abused by a preacher as a young girl. And now, every time I go to church, I remember."

A friend tells me that her husband cares more about his golf game than he cares about her.

Even as I was writing, a co-worker stopped by to update me on the lawsuit he has filed against the builder who never finished his house.

Is there anything wrong with these people? No, their desires are healthy. One wants a strong business, another wants fulfilling worship. A husband who'll honor his promise, a builder who'll keep his word. Who would fault them for such dreams? Who would blame them for dreaming? Who would have thought their dreams would be crushed?

Certainly they didn't.

But now they are faced with a decision. What do they do with their disillusionment? What do they do with their broken hearts? We're not talking inconveniences or hassles. We're not discussing long lines or red lights or a bad game of tennis. We're talking heartbreak. We're talking about what two friends of Jesus were feeling a couple of days after his death. Their world has tumbled in on them. It's obvious by the way they walk. Their feet shuffle, their heads hang, their shoulders droop. The seven miles from Jerusalem to Emmaus must feel like seventy.

As they walk they talk "about everything that had happened" (v. 14). It's not hard to imagine their words.

"Why did the people turn against him?"

"He could have come down from the cross. Why didn't he?"

"He just let Pilate push him around."

"What do we do now?"

As they walk, a stranger comes up behind them. It is Jesus, but they don't recognize him. Disappointment will do that to you. It will blind you to the very presence of God. Discouragement turns our eyes inward. God could be walking next to us, but despair clouds our vision.

Despair does something else. Not only does it cloud our vision, it hardens our hearts. We get cynical. We get calloused. And when good news comes, we don't want to accept it for fear of being disappointed again. That's what happened to these two people.

Later on they say these words:

And today some women among us amazed us. Early this morning they went to the tomb, but they did not find his body there. They came and told us that they had seen a vision of angels who said that Jesus was alive! So some of our group went to the tomb, too. They found it just as the women said, but they did not see Jesus.

Luke 24:22–24

When reading Scripture we can't always tell in what tone the words were spoken. Sometimes we don't know if the speaker means to be jubilant or sad or peaceful. This time, however, there is no question about what they're thinking: *As if it's not bad enough that Jesus was killed, now some grave robber has taken the body and duped some of our friends.*

These two followers aren't about to believe the women. Fool me once, shame on you. Fool me twice, shame on me. Cleopas and his friend are putting their hearts in a shell. They won't take another risk. They won't be hurt again.

Common reaction—isn't it? Been hurt by love? Then don't love. Had a promise violated? Then don't trust. Had your heart broken? Then don't give it away. Do like P. T. Barnum. Settle the score by blaming the world and hardening your heart.

There is a line, a fine line, which once crossed can be fatal. It's the line between disappointment and anger. Between hurt

87

and hate, between bitterness and blame. If you are nearing that line, let me urge you, don't cross it. Step back and ask this question: How long am I going to pay for my disappointment? How long am I going to go on nursing my hurt?

At some point you have to move on. At some point you have to heal. At some point you have to let Jesus do for you what he did for these men.

Know what he did? First of all, he came to them. I know we've already mentioned that, but it's worth repeating. He didn't sit back and cross his arms and say, "Why can't those two get with the program?" He didn't complain to the angel and say, "Why won't they believe the empty tomb? Why are they so hard to please?"

What did he do? He met them at their point of pain. Though death has been destroyed and sin annulled, he has not retired. The resurrected Lord has once again wrapped himself in flesh, put on human clothes, and searched out hurting hearts.

Read carefully their words and see if you can find their hurt:

> Jesus said to them, "What are you talking about?"
> They said, "About Jesus of Nazareth. He was a prophet who said and did many powerful things before God and all the people. Our leaders and the leading priests handed him over to be sentenced to death, and they crucified him. But we were hoping that he would free Israel."
>
> Luke 24:19–21

There it is. "But we were hoping . . ." The disciples had hoped Jesus would free Israel. They had hoped he'd kick out the Romans. They'd hoped Pilate would be out and Jesus would be in. But Pilate was still in, and Jesus was dead.

Unfulfilled expectations. God didn't do what they wanted him to.

They knew what they expected of Jesus. They knew what he was supposed to do. They didn't have to ask him. If Jesus is the Messiah, he won't sleep in my storm. He won't ever die. He won't defy tradition. He'll do what he is supposed to do.

But that's not what he did. And aren't we glad? Aren't we glad the prayer of Cleopas and his friend went unanswered? Aren't we glad God didn't adjust his agenda to fulfill the requests of these two disciples?

They were good disciples. With good hearts. And sincere prayers. They just had the wrong expectations.

When my oldest daughter was about six years old, she and I were having a discussion about my work. It seems she wasn't too happy with my chosen profession. She wanted me to leave the ministry. "I like you as a preacher," she explained. "I just really wish you sold snow cones."

An honest request from a pure heart. It made sense to her that the happiest people in the world were the men who drove the snow-cone trucks. You play music. You sell goodies. You make kids happy. What more could you want? (Come to think about it, she may have a point. I could get a loan, buy a truck and . . . Naw, I'd eat too much.)

I heard her request, but I didn't heed it. Why? Because I knew better. I know what I'm called to do and what I need to do. The fact is I know more about life than she does.

And the point is, God knows more about life than we do.

People wanted him to redeem Israel, but he knew better. He would rather his people be temporarily oppressed than eternally lost. When forced to choose between battling Pilate and battling Satan, he chose the battle we couldn't win. He said no to what they wanted and yes to what they needed. He said no to a liberated Israel and yes to a liberated humanity.

And once again, aren't we glad he did? And aren't we glad he does?

Now be honest. Are we glad he says no to what we want and yes to what we need? Not always. If we ask for a new marriage, and he says honor the one you've got, we aren't happy. If we ask for healing, and he says learn through the pain, we aren't happy. If we ask for more money, and he says treasure the unseen, we aren't always happy.

When God doesn't do what we want, it's not easy. Never has been. Never will be. But faith is the conviction that God knows more than we do about this life and he will get us through it.

Remember, disappointment is caused by unmet expectations. Disappointment is cured by revamped expectations.

I like that story about the fellow who went to the pet store in search of a singing parakeet. Seems he was a bachelor and his house was too quiet. The store owner had just the bird for him, so the man bought it. The next day the bachelor came home from work to a house full of music. He went to the cage to feed the bird and noticed for the first time that the parakeet had only one leg.

He felt cheated that he'd been sold a one-legged bird, so he called and complained.

"What do you want," the store owner responded, "a bird who can sing or a bird who can dance?"

Good question for times of disappointment. What do we want? That's what Jesus asks the disciples. What do you want? Do you want temporary freedom—or eternal freedom? Jesus sets about the task of restructuring their expectations.

You know what he did? He told them the story. Not just any story. He told them the story of God and God's plan for people. "Then starting with what Moses and all the prophets had said about him, Jesus began to explain everything that had been written about himself in the Scriptures" (v. 27).

Fascinating. Jesus' cure for the broken heart is the story of God. He started with Moses and finished with himself. Why did he do that? Why did he retell the ancient tale? Why did he go all the way back two thousand years to the story of Moses? I think I know the reason. I know because what they heard is what we all need to hear when we are disappointed.

We need to hear that God is still in control. We need to hear that it's not over until he says so. We need to hear that life's mishaps and tragedies are not a reason to bail out. They are simply a reason to sit tight.

Corrie ten Boom used to say, "When the train goes through a tunnel and the world gets dark, do you jump out? Of course not. You sit still and trust the engineer to get you through."

Why did Jesus tell the story? So we'd know the engineer still controls the train.

The way to deal with discouragement? The cure for disappointment? Go back to the story. Read it again and again. Be reminded that you aren't the first person to weep. And you aren't the first person to be helped.

Read the story and remember, their story is yours!

The challenge too great? Read the story. That's you crossing the Red Sea with Moses.

Too many worries? Read the story. That's you receiving heavenly food with the Israelites.

Your wounds too deep? Read the story. That's you, Joseph, forgiving your brothers for betraying you.

Your enemies too mighty? Read the story. That's you marching with Jehoshaphat into a battle already won.

Your disappointments too heavy? Read the story of the Emmaus-bound disciples. The Savior they thought was dead now walked beside them. He entered their house and sat at their table. And something happened in their hearts. "It felt like a fire burning in us when Jesus talked to us on the road and explained the Scriptures to us" (v. 31).

Next time you're disappointed, don't panic. Don't jump out. Don't give up. Just be patient and let God remind you he's still in control. It ain't over till it's over.

THE SMOLDERING WICK

Fibers interwoven for flame
Flame ignited for light
Cold gusts—hot blasts
Candle overcome by night
yet
Stubborn ember struggles
Duels with shadows and seeks
Brighter flame for power
Dancing fire for heat.

10

THE POWER OF
A TIMID PRAYER

When You Wonder If Your Prayers Matter

When Jesus, Peter, James, and John came back to the other followers, they saw a great crowd around them and the teachers of the law arguing with them. But as soon as the crowd saw Jesus, the people were surprised and ran to welcome him.

Jesus asked, "What are you arguing about?"

A man answered, "Teacher, I brought my son to you. He has an evil spirit in him that stops him from talking. When the spirit attacks him, it throws him on the ground. Then my son foams at the mouth, grinds his teeth, and becomes very stiff. I asked your followers to force the evil spirit out, but they couldn't."

Jesus answered, "You people have no faith. How long must I stay with you? How long must I put up with you? Bring the boy to me."

So the followers brought him to Jesus. As soon as the evil spirit saw Jesus, it made the boy lose control of himself, and he fell down and rolled on the ground, foaming at the mouth.

Jesus asked the boy's father, "How long has this been happening?"

The father answered, "Since he was very young. The spirit often throws him into a fire or into water to kill him. If you can do anything for him, please have pity on us and help us."

Jesus said to the father, "You said, 'If you can!' All things are possible for the one who believes."

Immediately the father cried out, "I do believe! Help me to believe more!"

When Jesus saw that a crowd was quickly gathering, he ordered the evil spirit, saying, "You spirit that makes people unable to hear or speak, I command you to come out of this boy and never enter him again!"

The evil spirit screamed and caused the boy to fall on the ground again. Then the spirit came out. The boy looked as if he were dead, and many people said, "He is dead!" But Jesus took hold of the boy's hand and helped him to stand up.

When Jesus went into the house, his followers began asking him privately, "Why couldn't we force that evil spirit out?"

Jesus answered, "That kind of spirit can only be forced out by prayer."

Mark 9:14–29

"That kind of spirit can only be forced out by prayer."

Mark 9:29

$\mathcal{T}$his chapter isn't for Concordes; it's for crop dusters.

Some of you pray like a Concorde jet—smooth, sleek, high, and mighty. Your words reverberate in the clouds and send sonic booms throughout the heavens. If you pray like a Concorde, I salute you. If you don't, I understand.

Maybe you are like me, more a crop duster than a Concorde. You aren't flashy, you fly low, you seem to cover the same ground a lot, and some mornings it's tough to get the old engine cranked up.

Most of us are like that. Most of our prayer lives could use a tune-up.

Some prayer lives lack consistency. They're either a desert or an oasis. Long, arid, dry spells interrupted by brief plunges into the waters of communion. We go days or weeks without consistent prayer, but then something happens—we hear a sermon, read a book, experience a tragedy—something leads us to pray, so we dive in. We submerge ourselves in prayer and leave refreshed and renewed. But as the journey resumes, our prayers don't.

Others of us need sincerity. Our prayers are a bit hollow, memorized, and rigid. More liturgy than life. And though they are daily, they are dull.

Still others lack, well, honesty. We honestly wonder if prayer makes a difference. Why on earth would God in heaven want to talk to me? If God knows all, who am I to tell him anything? If God controls all, who am I to do anything?

If you struggle with prayer, I've got just the guy for you. Don't worry, he's not a monastic saint. He's not a calloused-kneed apostle. Nor is he a prophet whose middle name is Meditation. He's not a too-holy-to-be-you reminder of how far you need to go in prayer. He's just the opposite. A fellow crop duster. A parent with a sick son in need of a miracle. The father's prayer isn't much, but the answer is and the result reminds us: The power is not in the prayer; it's in the one who hears it.

He prayed out of desperation. His son, his only son, was demon-possessed. Not only was he a deaf mute and an epileptic, he was also possessed by an evil spirit. Ever since the boy was young, the demon had thrown him into fires and water.

Imagine the pain of the father. Other dads could watch their children grow and mature; he could only watch his suffer. While others were teaching their sons an occupation, he was just trying to keep his son alive.

What a challenge! He couldn't leave his son alone for a minute. Who knew when the next attack would come? The father had to remain on call, on alert twenty-four hours a day. He was desperate and tired, and his prayer reflects both.

"If you can do anything for him, please have pity on us and help us."

Listen to that prayer. Does it sound courageous? Confident? Strong? Hardly.

One word would have made a lot of difference. Instead of *if,* what if he'd said *since?* "*Since* you can do anything for him, please have pity on us and help us."

But that's not what he said. He said *if.* The Greek is even more emphatic. The tense implies doubt. It's as if the man were saying, "This one's probably out of your league, but if you can . . ."

A classic crop-duster appeal. More meek than mighty. More timid than towering. More like a crippled lamb coming to a shepherd than a proud lion roaring in the jungle. If his prayer sounds like yours, then don't be discouraged, for that's where prayer begins.

It begins as a yearning. An honest appeal. Ordinary people staring at Mount Everest. No pretense. No boasting. No posturing. Just prayer. Feeble prayer, but prayer nonetheless.

We are tempted to wait to pray until we know how to pray. We've heard the prayers of the spiritually mature. We've read of the rigors of the disciplined. And we are convinced we've a long way to traverse.

And since we'd rather not pray than pray poorly, we don't pray. Or we pray infrequently. We are waiting to pray until we learn how to pray.

Good thing this man didn't make the same mistake. He wasn't much of a pray-er. And his wasn't much of a prayer. He even admits it! "I do believe," he implored. "Help me to believe more" (see Mark 9:24).

This prayer isn't destined for a worship manual. No Psalm will result from his utterance. His was simple—no incantation or chant. But Jesus responded. He responded, not to the eloquence of the man, but to the pain of the man.

Jesus had many reasons to disregard this man's request.

For one thing, Jesus was just returning from the mountain, the Mount of Transfiguration. While there his face had changed and his clothes had become as bright as a flash of lightning (see Luke 9:29). A roaring radiance had poured from him. The burdens of earth were replaced with the splendors of heaven. Moses and Elijah came and angels encouraged. He was lifted above the dusty horizon of Terra and invited into the sublime. He was transfigured. The journey up was exhilarating.

But the journey down was disheartening.

When we lived in Rio de Janeiro we would occasionally vacation in Teresopolis, a mountain village a couple of hours outside of the city. Teresopolis was everything Rio was not. It was quiet. It was clean. It was calm. And most of all it was cool. Rio was a sauna.

The trip down was always depressing. Poverty, heat, and pollution hit like a wave. We faced a herculean temptation to turn around and go back.

If Denalyn and I felt that way after a week in the mountains, imagine what Jesus must have felt after a glimpse into heaven!

Look at the chaos that greets him as he returns. The disciples and the religious leaders are arguing. A crowd of bystanders is gawking. A boy, who'd suffered all his life, is on public display. And a father who'd come for help is despondent, wondering why no one can help.

No wonder Jesus says, "You people have no faith. How long must I stay with you? How long must I put up with you?" (v. 19).

Never has the difference between heaven and earth been so stark.

Never has the arena of prayer been so poor. Where is the faith in this picture? The disciples have failed, the scribes are amused, the demon is victorious, and the father is desperate. You'd be hard-pressed to find a needle of belief in that haystack.

You may even be hard-pressed to find one in your own. Perhaps your life is a long way from heaven, too. Noisy household—screaming kids instead of singing angels. Divisive religion—your leaders squabble more than they minister. Overwhelming problems. You can't remember when you didn't wake up to this demon.

And yet out of the din of doubt comes your timid voice. "If you can do anything for me . . ."

Does such a prayer make a difference?

Let Mark answer that question.

When Jesus saw that a crowd was quickly gathering, he ordered the evil spirit, saying, "You spirit that makes people unable to hear or speak, I command you to come out of this boy and never enter him again."

> The evil spirit screamed and caused the boy to fall on the ground again. Then the spirit came out. The boy looked as if he were dead, and many people said, "He is dead!" But Jesus took hold of the boy's hand and helped him to stand up.
>
> Mark 9:25–27

This troubled the disciples. As soon as they got away from the crowds they asked Jesus, "Why couldn't we force that evil spirit out?"

His answer? "That kind of spirit can only be forced out by prayer." .

What prayer? What prayer made the difference? Was it the prayer of the apostles? No, they didn't pray. Must have been the prayers of the scribes. Maybe they went to the temple and interceded. No. The scribes didn't pray either. Then it must have been the people. Perhaps they had a vigil for the boy. Nope. The people didn't pray. They never bent a knee. Then what prayer led Jesus to deliver the demon?

There is only one prayer in the story. It's the honest prayer of a hurting man. And since God is more moved by our hurt than our eloquence, he responded. That's what fathers do.

That's exactly what Jim Redmond did.

His son Derek, a twenty-six-year-old Briton, was favored to win the four-hundred-meter race in the 1992 Barcelona Olympics. Halfway into his semifinal heat, a fiery pain seared through his right leg. He crumpled to the track with a torn hamstring.

As the medical attendants were approaching, Redmond fought to his feet. "It was animal instinct," he would later say. He set out hopping, pushing away the coaches in a crazed attempt to finish the race.

When he reached the stretch, a big man pushed through the crowd. He was wearing a t-shirt that read "Have you hugged your child today?" and a hat that challenged, "Just Do It." The man was Jim Redmond, Derek's father.

"You don't have to do this," he told his weeping son.

"Yes, I do," Derek declared.

"Well, then," said Jim, "we're going to finish this together."

And they did. Jim wrapped Derek's arm around his shoulder and helped him hobble to the finish line. Fighting off security men, the son's head sometimes buried in the father's shoulder, they stayed in Derek's lane to the end.

The crowd clapped, then stood, then cheered, and then wept as the father and son finished the race.

What made the father do it? What made the father leave the stands to meet his son on the track? Was it the strength of his child? No, it was the pain of his child. His son was hurt and fighting to complete the race. So the father came to help him finish.

God does the same. Our prayers may be awkward. Our attempts may be feeble. But since the power of prayer is in the one who hears it and not the one who says it, our prayers do make a difference.

11

BRIGHT LIGHTS ON
DARK NIGHTS

When You Are Out of Choices

Later Jesus went to Jerusalem for a special Jewish feast. In Jerusalem there is a pool with five covered porches, which is called Bethzatha in the Jewish language. This pool is near the Sheep Gate. Many sick people were lying on the porches beside the pool. Some were blind, some were crippled, and some were paralyzed. Sometimes an angel of the Lord came down to the pool and stirred up the water. After the angel did this, the first person to go into the pool was healed from any sickness he had. A man was lying there who had been sick for thirty-eight years. When Jesus saw the man and knew that he had been sick for such a long time, Jesus asked him, "Do you want to be well?"

The sick man answered, "Sir, there is no one to help me get into the pool when the water starts moving. While I am coming to the water, someone else always gets in before me."

Then Jesus said, "Stand up. Pick up your mat and walk." And immediately the man was well; he picked up his mat and began to walk.

The day this happened was a Sabbath day. So the Jews said to the man who had been healed, "Today is the Sabbath. It is against our law for you to carry your mat on the Sabbath day."

But he answered, "The man who made me well told me, 'Pick up your mat and walk.'"

Then they asked him, "Who is the man who told you to pick up your mat and walk?"

But the man who had been healed did not know who it was, because there were many people in that place, and Jesus had left.

Later, Jesus found the man at the Temple and said to him, "See, you are well now. Stop sinning so that something worse does not happen to you."

Then the man left and told the Jews that Jesus was the one who had made him well.

Because Jesus was doing this on the Sabbath day, the Jews began to persecute him. But Jesus said to them, "My Father never stops working, and so I keep working, too."

This made the Jews try still harder to kill him. They said, "First Jesus was breaking the law about the Sabbath day. Now he says that God is his own Father, making himself equal with God!"

John 5:1–18

> Jesus asked him, "Do you want to be well?"
>
> The sick man answered, "Sir, there is no one to help me."
>
> John 5:6–7

---

*F*or the longest time this story didn't make any sense to me. I couldn't figure it out. It's about a man who has barely enough faith to stand on, but Jesus treats him as if he'd laid his son on the altar for God. Martyrs and apostles deserve such honor, but not some pauper who doesn't know Jesus when he sees him. Or so I thought.

For the longest time I thought Jesus was too kind. I thought the story was too bizarre. I thought the story was too good to be true. Then I realized something. This story isn't about an invalid in Jerusalem. This story is about you. It's about me. The fellow isn't nameless. He has a name—yours. He has a face—mine. He has a problem—just like ours.

Jesus encounters the man near a large pool north of the temple in Jerusalem. It's 360 feet long, 130 feet wide, and 75 feet deep. A colonnade with five porches overlooks the body of water. It's a monument of wealth and prosperity, but its residents are people of sickness and disease.

It's called Bethesda. It could be called Central Park, Metropolitan Hospital, or even Joe's Bar and Grill. It could be the homeless huddled beneath a downtown overpass. It could be Calvary Baptist. It could be any collection of hurting people.

An underwater spring caused the pool to bubble occasionally. The people believed the bubbles were caused by the dipping of angels' wings. They also believed that the first person to touch the water after the angel did would be healed. Did healing occur? I don't know. But I do know crowds of invalids came to give it a try.

Picture a battleground strewn with wounded bodies, and you see Bethesda. Imagine a nursing home overcrowded and understaffed, and you see the pool. Call to mind the orphans in Bangladesh or the abandoned in New Delhi, and you will see what people saw when they passed Bethesda. As they passed, what did they hear? An endless wave of groans. What did they witness? A field of faceless need. What did they do? Most walked past, ignoring the people.

But not Jesus. He is in Jerusalem for a feast. We don't know if he ever made it to the temple, but we do know he made it to Bethesda.

He is alone. He's not there to teach the disciples or to draw a crowd. The people need him—so he's there.

Can you picture it? Jesus walking among the suffering.

What is he thinking? When an infected hand touches his ankle, what does he do? When a blind child stumbles in Jesus' path, does he reach down to catch the child? When a wrinkled hand extends for alms, how does Jesus respond?

Whether the watering hole is Bethesda or Bill's Bar . . . how does God feel when people hurt?

It's worth the telling of the story if all we do is watch him walk. It's worth it just to know he even came. He didn't have to, you know. Surely there are more sanitary crowds in Jerusalem. Surely there are more enjoyable activities. After all, this is the Passover feast. It's an exciting time in the holy city. People have come from miles around to meet God in the temple.

Little do they know that God is with the sick.

Little do they know that God is walking slowly, stepping carefully between the beggars and the blind.

Little do they know that the strong young carpenter who surveys the ragged landscape of pain is God.

"When they suffered, he suffered also" Isaiah wrote (Isa. 63:9). On this day Jesus must have suffered much.

On this day Jesus must have sighed often as he walked along the poolside of Bethesda . . . and he sighs when he comes to you and me.

Remember, I told you this story was about us? Remember, I said I found our faces in the Bible? Well, here we are, filling the white space between the letters of verse 5: "A man was lying there who had been sick for thirty-eight years."

Maybe you don't like being described like that. Perhaps you'd rather find yourself in the courage of David or the devotion of Mary. We all would. But before you or I can be like them, we must admit we are like the paralytic. Invalids out of options. Can't walk. Can't work. Can't care for ourselves. Can't even roll down the bank to the pool to cash in on the angel water.

You may be holding this book with healthy hands and reading with strong eyes, and you can't imagine what you and this four-decade invalid have in common. How could he be you? What do we have in common with him?

Simple. Our predicament and our hope. What predicament? It is described in Hebrews 12:14: "Anyone whose life is not holy will never see the Lord."

That's our predicament: Only the holy will see God. Holiness is a prerequisite to heaven. Perfection is a requirement for eternity. We wish it weren't so. We act like it isn't so. We act like those who are "decent" will see God. We suggest that those who try hard will see God. We act as if we're good if we never do anything too bad. And that goodness is enough to qualify us for heaven.

Sounds right to us, but it doesn't sound right to God. And he sets the standard. And the standard is high. "You must be perfect, just as your Father in heaven is perfect" (Matt. 5:48).

You see, in God's plan, God is the standard for perfection. We don't compare ourself to others; they are just as fouled up as we are. The goal is to be like him; anything less is inadequate.

That's why I say the invalid is you and me. We, like the invalid, are paralyzed. We, like the invalid, are trapped. We, like the invalid, are stuck; we have no solution for our predicament.

That's you and me lying on the ground. That's us wounded and weary. When it comes to healing our spiritual condition, we don't have a chance. We might as well be told to pole-vault the moon. We don't have what it takes to be healed. Our only hope is that God will do for us what he did for the man at Bethesda—that he will step out of the temple and step into our ward of hurt and helplessness.

Which is exactly what he has done.

Read slowly and carefully Paul's description of what God has done for you: "When you were spiritually dead because of your sins and because you were not free from the power of your sinful self, God made you alive with Christ, and he forgave all our sins. He canceled the debt, which listed all the rules we failed to follow. He took away that record with its rules and nailed it to the cross. God stripped the spiritual rulers and powers of their authority. With the cross, he won the victory and showed the world that they were powerless" (Col. 2:13–15).

As you look at the words above, answer this question. Who is doing the work? You or God? Who is active? You or God? Who is doing the saving? You or God? Who is the one with strength? And who is the one paralyzed?

Let's isolate some phrases and see. First, look at your condition. "When you were spiritually dead . . . and . . . you were not free."

The invalid was better off than we are. At least he was alive. Paul says that if you and I are outside of Christ, then we are dead. Spiritually dead. Corpses. Lifeless. Cadavers. Dead. What can a dead person do? Not much.

But look what God can do with the dead.

> "God made you alive."
>
> "God forgave."
>
> "He canceled the debt."
>
> "He took away that record."

"God stripped the spiritual rulers."

"He won the victory."

"[He] showed the world."

Again, the question. Who is active? You and I—or God? Who is trapped and who comes to the rescue?

God has thrown life jackets to every generation.

Look at Jonah in the fish belly—surrounded by gastric juices and sucked-in seaweed. For three days God has left him there. For three days Jonah has pondered his choices. And for three days he has come to the same conclusion: He ain't got one. From where he sits (or floats) there are two exits—and neither are very appealing. But then again, neither is Jonah. He blew it as a preacher. He was a flop as a fugitive. At best he's a coward, at worst a traitor. And what he's lacked all along he now has in abundance—guts.

So Jonah does the only thing he can do: He prays. He says nothing about how good he is—but a lot about how good God is. He doesn't even ask for help, but help is what he gets. Before he can say amen, the belly convulses, the fish belches, and Jonah lands face first on the beach.

Look at Daniel in the lions' den; his prospects aren't much better than Jonah's. Jonah had been swallowed, and Daniel is about to be. Flat on his back with the lions' faces so close he can smell their breath. The biggest one puts a paw on Daniel's chest and leans down to take the first bite and . . . nothing happens. Instead of a chomp, there is a bump. Daniel looks down and sees the nose of another lion rubbing against his belly. The lion's lips are snarling, but his mouth isn't opening.

That's when Daniel hears the snickering in the corner. He doesn't know who the fellow is, but he sure is bright and he sure is having fun. In his hands is a roll of bailing wire and on his face is one of those gotcha-while-you-weren't-watching expressions.

Or look at Joseph in the pit, a chalky hole in a hot desert. The lid has been pulled over the top and the wool has been pulled over his eyes. Those are his brothers up there, laughing and eating as if they did nothing more than tell him to get lost (which is what they'd done for most of his life). Those are his brothers, the ones who have every intention of leaving him to spend his days with the spiders and the snakes and then to die in the pit.

Like Jonah and Daniel, Joseph is trapped. He is out of options. There is no exit. There is no hope. But because Jacob's boys are as greedy as they were mean, Joseph is sold to some southbound gypsies and he changes history. Though the road to the palace takes a detour through a prison, it eventually ends up at the throne. And Joseph eventually stands before his brothers—this time with their asking for his help. And he is wise enough to give them what they ask and not what they deserve.

Or look at Barabbas on death row. The final appeal has been heard. The execution has been scheduled. Barabbas passes the time playing solitaire in his cell. He's resigned to the fact that the end is near. Doesn't appeal. Doesn't implore. Doesn't demand. The decision has been made, and Barabbas is going to die.

Like Jonah, Daniel, and Joseph, it's all over but the crying. And like Jonah, Daniel, and Joseph, the time to cry never comes. The steps of the warden echo in the chamber. Barabbas thinks he's bringing handcuffs and a final cigarette. Wrong. The warden brings street clothes. And Barabbas leaves the prison a free man because someone he'd probably never even seen took his place.

Such are the stories in the Bible. One near-death experience after another. Just when the neck is on the chopping block, just when the noose is around the neck, Calvary comes.

Angels pound on Lot's door—Genesis 19.
The whirlwind speaks to Job's hurt—Job 38–42.
The Jordan purges Naaman's plague—2 Kings 5.
An angel appears in Peter's cell—Acts 12.

God's efforts are strongest when our efforts are useless.

Go back to Bethesda for a moment. I want you to look at the brief but revealing dialogue between the paralytic and the

Savior. Before Jesus heals him, he asks him a question: "Do you want to be well?"

"Sir, there is no one to help me get into the pool when the water starts moving. While I am coming to the water, someone else always gets in before me" (v. 7).

Is the fellow complaining? Is he feeling sorry for himself? Or is he just stating the facts? Who knows. But before we think about it too much, look what happens next.

"'Stand up. Pick up your mat and walk.'"

"And immediately the man was well; he picked up his mat and began to walk."

I wish we would do that; I wish we would take Jesus at his word. I wish, like heaven, that we would learn that when he says something, it happens. What is this peculiar paralysis that confines us? What is this stubborn unwillingness to be healed? When Jesus tells us to stand, let's stand.

> When he says we're forgiven, let's unload the guilt.
> When he says we're valuable, let's believe him.
> When he says we're eternal, let's bury our fear.
> When he says we're provided for, let's stop worrying.
> When he says, "Stand up," let's do it.

I love the story of the private who ran after and caught the runaway horse of Alexander the Great. When he brought the animal back to the general, Alexander thanked him by saying, "Thank you, captain."

With one word the private was promoted. When the general said it, the private believed it. He went to the quartermaster, selected a new uniform, and put it on. He went to the officers' quarters and selected a bunk. He went to the officers' mess and had a meal.

Because the general said it, he believed it. Would that we would do the same.

Is this your story? It can be. All the elements are the same. A gentle stranger has stepped into your hurting world and offered you a hand.

Now it's up to you to take it.

12

THE HARDEST THING GOD EVER DID

Understanding God's Priority

A few days later, when Jesus came back to Capernaum, the news spread that he was at home. Many people gathered together so that there was no room in the house, not even outside the door. And Jesus was teaching them God's message. Four people came, carrying a paralyzed man. Since they could not get to Jesus because of the crowd, they dug a hole in the roof right above where he was speaking. When they got through, they lowered the mat with the paralyzed man on it. When Jesus saw the faith of these people, he said to the paralyzed man, "Young man, your sins are forgiven."

Some of the teachers of the law were sitting there, thinking to themselves, "Why does this man say things like that? He is speaking as if he were God. Only God can forgive sins."

Jesus knew immediately what these teachers of the law were thinking. So he said to them, "Why are you thinking these things? Which is easier: to tell this paralyzed man, 'Your sins are forgiven,' or to tell him, 'Stand up. Take your mat and walk'? But I will prove to you that the Son of Man has authority on earth to forgive sins." So Jesus said to the paralyzed man, "I tell you, stand up, take your mat, and go home." Immediately the paralyzed man stood up, took his mat, and walked out while everyone was watching him.

The people were amazed and praised God. They said, "We have never seen anything like this!"

Mark 2:1–12

> "Which is easier: to tell this paralyzed
> man, 'Your sins are forgiven,' or to tell
> him, 'Stand up. Take your mat and
> walk'?"
>
> Mark 2:9

_____

*L*et's talk for a minute about lovebursts.

You've witnessed *sunbursts:* sunlight shafting into a shadowed forest. You've seen *starbursts:* shots of light soaring through a night sky. And you've heard *powerbursts:* raw energy booming in the silence. And you've felt *lovebursts.* You may not have called them such, but you've felt them.

Lovebursts. Spontaneous affection. Tender moments of radiant love. Ignited devotion. Explosions of tenderness. May I illustrate?

You and your husband are at a party. One of those stand-in-the-living-room-and-talk-and-eat parties. You are visiting with some women, and your husband is across the room in a circle of men. The topic in your group is husbands, and the collective opinion is negative. The women complain about the amount of golf, dirty socks, and late nights at work. But you're silent. You say little because you have little to say. The guy you married isn't perfect, but he isn't a pain either. In fact, compared to these guys, he sounds pretty special. He's changed more than his share of diapers, and his golf clubs haven't come down out of the attic since the last baby was born. You look across the room at your husband and smile at the way he tugs at the tie you convinced him to wear. Still as handsome as the day you met. A bit paunchier and balder perhaps, but you don't see that. All you see is the man who stole your heart. And all of a sudden you'd go to China in a rowboat to tell him how glad you are that he did.

That's a loveburst. Here is another.

It's been a while since you held a baby. It's been a while since you were near a baby. But now you're alone with the baby. Your kids dropped him off at the house for the evening, and your wife ran to the store to get some milk, and now it's just you and your grandson. He's only a few days old and wrapped tighter than the cigars you gave your friends. As you cradle him in your arms, you realize this is the first time the two of you have been alone. With all the fanfare and friends at the hospital, you haven't shared a private moment—till now. So you sit in your big chair and turn him so you can see his face. You ponder the future, his future: first steps, first kiss, football, college. You wonder what it's going to be like being a kid in a world where hurt seems to linger on every corner.

As you look into the little eyes and nose that came from the other side of the family, it hits you. Out of nowhere comes a bolt of devotion. You're suddenly aware that hell itself would have to get past you to get to this one who carries your name. "It's gonna be all right," you hear yourself pledge to the sleeping boy. "Whatever happens, just remember I'm here. It's gonna be all right."

May I share one more?

You came home cranky because a deadline got moved up. She came home grumpy because the day care forgot to give your five-year-old her throat medicine. Each of you was wanting a little sympathy from the other, but neither got any. So there you sit at the dinner table—cranky and grumpy—with little Emily. Emily folds her hands to pray (as she has been taught), and the two of you bow you heads (but not your hearts) and listen. From where this prayer comes, God only knows.

"God, it's Emily. How are you? I'm fine, thank you. Mom and Dad are mad. I don't know why. We've got birds and toys and mash potatoes and each other. Maybe you can get them to stop being mad? Please do, or it's just gonna be you and me having any fun tonight. Amen."

The prayer is answered before it's finished; you both look up in the middle and laugh at the end and shake your heads and say you're sorry. And you both thank God for the little voice who reminded you about what matters.

That's what lovebursts do. They remind you about what matters. A telegram delivered to the back door of the familiar, telling you to treasure the treasure you've got while you've got it. A whisper from an angel, or someone who sounds like one, reminding you that what you have is greater than what you want and that what is urgent is not always what matters.

Those are lovebursts. You have them. I have them. And this may surprise you: Jesus had them . . . lots of them.

One of them happened when Jesus met an invalid. The man couldn't walk. He couldn't stand. His limbs were bent and his body twisted. A waist-high world walked past as he sat and watched.

Perhaps he was palsied, his body ridden with disease since birth. While other children had jumped and run, he had labored to bring a spoon to his mouth. As his brothers and sisters spoke and sang, his words slurred and slipped. Maybe he had never known what it was to be whole.

Or maybe he had known. Maybe he had once been healthy. Was there a time when he was known for his ability, not his disability? Was there an era when he could outrun anyone? Was there a time when he was the strongest in the shop? Was there a day when every kid in the village wanted to be like him?

Then came the fall—a tumble down a canyon, perhaps a stumble down some stairs. The pain in his skull was unbearable, but the numbness in his legs and arms was far worse. His feet hung like ornaments on the ends of his legs. His hands dangled like empty sleeves from his sides. He could see his limbs, but he couldn't feel them.

Whether he was born paralyzed or became paralyzed—the end result was the same: total dependence on others. Someone had to wash his face and bathe his body. He couldn't blow his nose or go on a walk. When he ran, it was in his dreams, and his dreams would always awaken to a body that couldn't roll over and couldn't go back to sleep for all the hurt the night dream had brought.

"What he needs is a new body," any man in half his mind would say. What he needs is a God in heaven to restore what tragedy has robbed: arms that swing, hands that grip, and feet that dance.

When people looked at him, they didn't see the man; they saw a body in need of a miracle. That's not what people saw, but that's what the people saw. And that's certainly what his friends saw. So they did what any of us would do for a friend. They tried to get him some help.

Word was out that a carpenter-turned-teacher-turned-wonder-worker was in town. And as the word got out, the people came. They came from every hole and hovel in Israel. They came like soldiers returning from battle—bandaged, crippled, sightless. The old with prune faces and toothless mouths. The young with deaf babies and broken hearts. Fathers with sons who couldn't speak. Wives with wombs that wouldn't bear fruit. The world, it seemed, had come to see if he was real or right or both.

By the time his friends arrived at the place, the house was full. People jammed the doorways. Kids sat in the windows. Others peeked over shoulders. How would this small band of friends ever attract Jesus' attention? They had to make a choice: Do we go in or give up?

What would have happened had the friends given up? What if they had shrugged their shoulders and mumbled something about the crowd being big and dinner getting cold and turned and left? After all, they had done a good deed in coming this far. Who could fault them for turning back? You can only do so much for somebody. But these friends hadn't done enough.

One said that he had an idea. The four huddled over the paralytic and listened to the plan to climb to the top of the house, cut through the roof, and lower their friend down with their sashes.

It was risky—they could fall. It was dangerous—*he* could fall. It was unorthodox—de-roofing is antisocial. It was intrusive—Jesus was busy. But it was their only chance to see Jesus. So they climbed to the roof.

Faith does those things. Faith does the unexpected. And faith gets God's attention. Look what Mark says: "When Jesus saw the faith of these people, he said to the paralyzed man, 'Young man, your sins are forgiven'" (v. 5).

Finally, someone took him at his word! Four men had enough hope in him and love for their friend that they took a chance. The stretcher above was a sign from above—somebody believes! Someone was willing to risk embarrassment and injury for just a few moments with the Galilean.

Jesus was moved.

> Like the wife overwhelmed with love for her paunchy but precious husband.
>
> Like the grandfather determined to protect his grandson.
>
> Like the parents touched by the prayer of their child.

Jesus was moved by the scene of faith. So he applauds—if not with his hands, at least with his heart. And not only does he applaud, he blesses. And we witness a divine loveburst.

The friends want him to heal their friend. But Jesus won't settle for a simple healing of the body—he wants to heal the soul. He leapfrogs the physical and deals with the spiritual. To heal the body is temporal; to heal the soul is eternal.

The request of the friends is valid—but timid. The expectations of the crowd are high—but not high enough. They expect Jesus to say, "I heal you." Instead he says, "I forgive you."

They expect him to treat the body, for that is what they see.

He chooses to treat not only the body, but also the spiritual, for that is what he sees.

They want Jesus to give the man a new body so he can walk. Jesus gives grace so the man can live.

Remarkable. Sometimes God is so touched by what he sees that he gives us what we need and not simply that for which we ask.

It's a good thing. For who would have ever thought to ask God for what he gives? Which of us would have dared to say: "God, would you please hang yourself on a tool of torture as a substitution for every mistake I have ever committed?" And then have the audacity to add: "And after you forgive me, could you prepare me a place in your house to live forever?"

And if that wasn't enough: "And would you please live within me and protect me and guide me and bless me with more than I could ever deserve?"

Honestly, would we have the chutzpah to ask for that? No, we, like the friends, would have only asked for the small stuff.

We would ask for little things like a long life and a healthy body and a good job. Grand requests from our perspective, but from God's it's like taking the moped when he offers the limo.

So, knowing the paralytic didn't know enough to ask for what he needed, Jesus gave it anyway: "Young man, your sins are forgiven" (v. 5).

The Pharisees start to grumble. That's not kosher. Even a tenderfoot Jew knows, "Only God can forgive sins" (v. 7).

Their mumbling spawns one of Christ's greatest questions: "Which is easier: to tell this paralyzed man, 'Your sins are forgiven,' or to tell him, 'Stand up. Take your mat and walk'?" (v. 9).

You answer the question. Which is easier for Jesus? To forgive a soul or heal a body? Which caused Jesus less pain—providing this man with health or providing this man with heaven?

To heal the man's body took a simple command; to forgive the man's sins took Jesus' blood. The first was done in the house of friends; the second on a hill with thieves. One took a word; the other took his body. One took a moment; the other took his life.

Which was easier?

So strong was his love for this crew of faith that he went beyond their appeal and went straight to the cross.

Jesus already knows the cost of grace. He already knows the price of forgiveness. But he offers it anyway. Love burst his heart.

By the way, he hasn't changed. What happened then happens today. When we take a step of faith, God sees. The same face that beamed at the paralytic beams at the alcoholic refusing the bottle. The same eyes that danced at the friends dance at the mom and dad who will do whatever it takes to get their child to Jesus. And the same lips that spoke to the man in Capernaum speak to the man in Detroit, to the woman in Belfast, to the child in Moscow . . . to any person anywhere who dares to come into the presence of God and ask for help.

And though we can't hear it here, the angels can hear him there. All of heaven must pause as another burst of love declares the only words that really matter: "Your sins are forgiven."

13

WHAT ONLY GOD CAN DO

When You're Trapped by Legalism

There was a man named Nicodemus who was one of the Pharisees and an important Jewish leader. One night Nicodemus came to Jesus and said, "Teacher, we know you are a teacher sent from God, because no one can do the miracles you do unless God is with him."

Jesus answered, "I tell you the truth, unless one is born again, he cannot be in God's kingdom."

Nicodemus said, "But if a person is already old, how can he be born again? He cannot enter his mother's body again. So how can a person be born a second time?"

But Jesus answered, "I tell you the truth, unless one is born from water and the Spirit, he cannot enter God's kingdom. Human life comes from human parents, but spiritual life comes from the Spirit. Don't be surprised when I tell you, 'You must all be born again.' The wind blows where it wants to and you hear the sound of it, but you don't know where the wind comes from or where it is going. It is the same with every person who is born from the Spirit."

Nicodemus asked, "How can this happen?"

Jesus said, "You are an important teacher in Israel, and you don't understand these things? I tell you the truth, we talk about what we know, and we tell about what we have seen, but you don't accept what we tell you. I have told you about things here on earth, and you do not believe me. So you will not believe me if I tell you about things of heaven. The only one who has ever gone up to heaven is the One who came down from heaven—the Son of Man.

"Just as Moses lifted up the snake in the desert, the Son of Man must also be lifted up. So that everyone who believes can have eternal life in him.

"God loved the world so much that he gave his one and only Son so that whoever believes in him may not be lost, but have eternal life. God did not send his Son into the world to judge the world guilty, but to save the world through him. People who

believe in God's Son are not judged guilty. Those who do not
believe have already been judged guilty, because they have not
believed in God's one and only Son. They are judged by this
fact: The Light has come into the world, but they did not want
light. They wanted darkness, because they were doing evil
things. All who do evil hate the light and will not come to the
light, because it will show all the evil things they do. But those
who follow the true way come to the light, and it shows that the
things they do were done through God."

John 3:1–21

But Jesus answered, "I tell you the truth, unless one is born from water and the Spirit, he cannot enter God's kingdom."

John 3:5

---

*I*t's a fact of the farm. The most fertile ground remains barren if no seed is sown.

Apparently Nicodemus didn't know that. He thought the soil could bear fruit with no seeds. He was big on the farmer's part but forgetful of the seed's part. He was a legalist. And that is how a legalist thinks. A legalist prepares the soil but forgets the seed.

Nicodemus came about his legalism honestly. He was a Pharisee.

Pharisees taught that faith was an outside job. What you wore, how you acted, the title you carried, the sound of your prayers, the amount of your gifts—all these were the Pharisees' measure of spirituality.

Had they been farmers, they would have had the most attractive acreage in the region—painted silos and sparkling equipment. The fences would have been whitewashed and clean. The soil overturned and watered.

Had they been farmers they would have spent hours in the coffee shop discussing the theory of farming. Is it best to fertilize before or after a rain? Do you fallow a field every other year or every third year? Should a farmer wear overalls or jeans? Cowboy hats or baseball caps?

The Pharisees had only one problem. For all their discussion about the right techniques, they harvested little fruit. In fact, one untrained Galilean had borne more fruit in a few short months than all the Pharisees had in a generation. This made them jealous. Angry. Condescending. And they dealt with him by ignoring his results and insulting his methods.

That is, all the Pharisees except Nicodemus. He was curious. No, more than curious, he was stirred; stirred by the way people listened to Jesus. They listened as if he were the only one with truth. As if he were a prophet.

Nicodemus was stirred by what he saw Jesus do. Like the time Jesus stormed into the temple and overturned the tables of the moneychangers. Nicodemus once knew such passion. But that was a long time ago—before the titles, before the robes, before the rules.

Nicodemus is drawn to the carpenter, but he can't be seen with him. Nicodemus is on the high court. He can't approach Jesus in the day. So Nicodemus goes to meet him at night. He goes in the darkness.

Appropriate. For legalism offers no light.

Nicodemus begins with courtesies, "Teacher, we know you are a teacher sent from God, because no one can do the miracles you do unless God is with him" (v. 2).

Jesus disregards the compliment. "I tell you the truth, unless one is born again, he cannot be in God's kingdom" (v. 3).

No chitchat here. No idle talk. Straight to the point. Straight to the heart. Straight to the problem. Jesus knows the heart of the legalist is hard. You can't crack it with feathery accolades. You need a chisel. So Jesus hammers away:

> You can't help the blind by turning up the light, Nicodemus.
>
> You can't help the deaf by turning up the music, Nicodemus.
>
> You can't change the inside by decorating the outside, Nicodemus.
>
> You can't grow fruit without seed, Nicodemus.

You must be born again.

Whack! Whack! Whack!

The meeting between Jesus and Nicodemus was more than an encounter between two religious figures. It was a collision between two philosophies. Two opposing views on salvation.

Nicodemus thought the person did the work; Jesus says God does the work. Nicodemus thought it was a tradeoff. Jesus says it is a gift. Nicodemus thought man's job was to earn it. Jesus says man's job is to accept it.

These two views encompass all views. All the world religions can be placed in one of two camps: legalism or grace. Humankind does it or God does it. Salvation as a wage based on deeds done—or salvation as a gift based on Christ's death.

A legalist believes the supreme force behind salvation is you. If you look right, speak right, and belong to the right segment of the right group, you will be saved. The brunt of responsibility doesn't lie within God; it lies within you.

The result? The outside sparkles. The talk is good and the step is true. But look closely. Listen carefully. Something is missing. What is it? Joy. What's there? Fear. (That you won't do enough.) Arrogance. (That you have done enough.) Failure. (That you have made a mistake.)

Legalism is a dark world.

Perhaps you didn't know that. You may be reading with a puzzled expression asking, "What is this story doing in this book, Max? I thought this was a book about Jesus meeting people at their point of pain. Nicodemus isn't hurting. He's got clout. He's got friends. He studies the Bible. He's not in pain, is he?"

If you asked that question, be thankful. If you have never known the crush of legalism, be grateful. You have been spared.

Others of you haven't. Others of you could answer the above question better than I. Legalism is slow torture, suffocation of the spirit, amputation of one's dreams. Legalism is just enough religion to keep you, but not enough to nourish you.

So you starve. Your teachers don't know where to go for food, so you starve together. Your diet is rules and standards. No vitamins. No taste. No zest. Just bland, predictable religion.

Reminds me of a group I was in as a youngster. When I was eight years old I was a part of a boys' choir. We met two evenings a week for two hours. We wore blazers and sang at banquets. We even went on the road.

Curiously, our instructor was an ex-drill sergeant. Before he ran a boys' choir, he ran a boot camp. And some of the previous spilled over into the latter. Every evening during rehearsals, we took a marching break. We'd go outside and march in formation. He gave the commands, and we did the turns.

"Hut, two, three, four. Hut, two, three, four."

At first, I didn't question the practice. I didn't have the courage. I was intimidated by the man. Finally, I summoned enough guts to ask the kid beside me to explain the marching.

"Why are we doing this?"

"I don't know."

"Where are we going?"

"I don't know."

No one did. For two years we marched two nights every week. But no one knew where we were going and no one knew why. We just knew that if we wanted to sing we'd better stay in step.

That's legalism.

It's rigid. It's uniform. It's mechanical—and it's not from God.

Can I give you the down and dirty about legalism?

Legalism doesn't need God. Legalism is the search for innocence—not forgiveness. It's a systematic process of defending self, explaining self, exalting self, and justifying self. Legalists are obsessed with self—not God.

Legalism:

> Turns my opinion into your burden. There is only room for one opinion in this boat. And guess who is wrong!
>
> Turns my opinion into your boundary. Your opposing opinion makes me question not only your right to have fellowship with me, but also your salvation.

129

Turns my opinion into your obligation. Christians must
    toe the company line. Your job isn't to think, it's
    to march.

If you want to be in the group, stay in step and don't ask questions.

Nicodemus knew how to march, but he longed to sing. He knew there was something more, but he didn't know where to find it. So he went to Jesus.

He went at night because he feared the displeasure of his peers. Legalism puts the fear of man in you. It makes you approval-hungry. You become keenly aware of what others will say and think, and you do what it takes to please them. Conformity is not fun, but it's safe. The uniform doesn't fit, but it's approved, so you wear it. You don't know why you are marching or where you are going—but who are you to ask questions? So you stay in step and plod down the path of least resistance.

And if you dare explore another trail, you must do so at night, like Nicodemus did. He snuck through the shadows and crept through the ebony streets until he stood in the presence of Christ. In the conversation, Nicodemus, the renowned teacher of the law, speaks only three times: once to compliment and twice to question. After a lifetime of weighing the tittles of Scripture in the scale of logic, the scholar becomes suddenly silent as Jesus opens the gate and the light of grace floods the catacomb.

Jesus begins by revealing the source of spirituality: "Human life comes from human parents, but spiritual life comes from the Spirit" (v. 6).

Spiritual life is not a human endeavor. It is rooted in and orchestrated by the Holy Spirit. Every spiritual achievement is created and energized by God.

Spirituality, Jesus says, comes not from church attendance or good deeds or correct doctrine, but from heaven itself. Such words must have set Nicodemus back on his heels. But Jesus was just getting started.

"The wind blows where it wants to and you hear the sound of it, but you don't know where the wind comes from or where it is going. It is the same with every person who is born from the Spirit" (v. 8).

Ever had a gust of wind come to you for help? Ever seen a windstorm on the side of the road catching its breath? No, you haven't. The wind doesn't seek our aid. Wind doesn't even reveal its destiny. It's silent and invisible and so is the Spirit.

By now Nicodemus was growing edgy. Such light is too bright for his eyes. We religious teachers like to control and manage. We like to define and outline. Structure and clarity are the friend of the preacher. But they aren't always the protocol of God.

Salvation is God's business. Grace is his idea, his work, and his expense. He offers it to whom he desires, when he desires. Our job in the process is to inform the people, not to screen the people.

The question must have been written all over Nicodemus's face. Why would God do this? What would motivate him to offer such a gift? What Jesus told Nicodemus, Nicodemus never could have imagined. The motive behind the gift of new birth? Love. "God loved the world so much that he gave his one and only Son so that whoever believes in him may not be lost, but have eternal life (v. 16).

Nicodemus has never heard such words. Never. He has had many discussions of salvation. But this is the first in which no rules were given. No system was offered. No code or ritual. "Everyone who believes can have eternal life in him," Jesus told him. Could God be so generous? Even in the darkness of night, the amazement is seen on Nicodemus's face. *Everyone who believes can have eternal life.* Not "everyone who achieves." Not "everyone who succeeds." Not "everyone who agrees." But "everyone who believes."

Note how God liberates the legalist. Observe the tender firmness of his touch. Like a master farmer, he shoveled away the crusty soil until a moist, fertile spot was found, and there he planted a seed, a seed of grace.

Did it bear fruit? Read the following and see for yourself.

131

Nicodemus, who earlier had come to Jesus at night, went with Joseph. He brought about seventy-five pounds of myrrh and aloes. These two men took Jesus' body and wrapped it with the spices in pieces of linen cloth, which is how Jewish people bury the dead. In the place where Jesus was crucified, there was a garden. In the garden was a new tomb that had never been used before. The men laid Jesus in that tomb.

John 19:39–42

Strange how a man can go full circle in the kingdom. The one who'd come at night now appears in the day. The one who crept through the shadows to meet Jesus now comes to the cross to serve Jesus. And the one who'd received the seed of grace now plants the greatest seed of all—the seed of eternal life.

14

GALILEAN GRACE

When You Let God Down

Later, Jesus showed himself to his followers again—this time at Lake Galilee. This is how he showed himself: Some of the followers were together: Simon Peter, Thomas (called Didymus), Nathanael from Cana in Galilee, the two sons of Zebedee, and two other followers. Simon Peter said, "I am going out to fish."

The others said, "We will go with you." So they went out and got into the boat. They fished that night but caught nothing.

Early the next morning Jesus stood on the shore, but the followers did not know it was Jesus. Then he said to them, "Friends, did you catch any fish?"

They answered, "No."

He said, "Throw your net on the right side of the boat, and you will find some." So they did, and they caught so many fish they could not pull the net back into the boat.

The follower whom Jesus loved said to Peter, "It is the Lord!" When Peter heard him say this, he wrapped his coat around himself. (Peter had taken his clothes off.) Then he jumped into the water. The other followers went to shore in the boat, dragging the net full of fish. They were not very far from shore, only about a hundred yards. When the followers stepped out of the boat and onto the shore, they saw a fire of hot coals. There were fish on the fire, and there was bread.

Then Jesus said, "Bring some of the fish you just caught."

Simon Peter went into the boat and pulled the net to the shore. It was full of big fish, one hundred fifty-three in all, but even though there were so many, the net did not tear.

John 21:1–11

> The follower whom Jesus loved said
> to Peter, "It is the Lord!" When Peter
> heard him say this, he wrapped his
> coat around himself. (Peter had taken
> his clothes off.) Then he jumped into
> the water.
>
> John 21:7

The sun was in the water before Peter noticed it—a wavy circle of gold on the surface of the sea. A fisherman is usually the first to spot the sun rising over the crest of the hills. It means his night of labor is finally over.

But not for this fisherman. Though the light reflected on the lake, the darkness lingered in Peter's heart. The wind chilled, but he didn't feel it. His friends slept soundly, but he didn't care. The nets at his feet were empty, the sea had been a miser, but Peter wasn't thinking about that.

His thoughts were far from the Sea of Galilee. His mind was in Jerusalem, reliving an anguished night. As the boat rocked, his memories raced:

> the clanking of the Roman guard,
> the flash of a sword and the duck of a head,
> a touch for Malchus, a rebuke for Peter,
> soldiers leading Jesus away.

"What was I thinking?" Peter mumbled to himself as he stared at the bottom of the boat. *Why did I run?*

Peter had run; he had turned his back on his dearest friend and run. We don't know where. Peter may not have known where. He found a hole, a hut, an abandoned shed—he found a place to hide and he hid.

He had bragged, "Everyone else may stumble . . . but I will not" (Matt. 26:33). Yet he did. Peter did what he swore he wouldn't do. He had tumbled face first into the pit of his own fears. And there he sat. All he could hear was his hollow promise. *Everyone else may stumble . . . but I will not. Everyone else . . . I will not. I will not. I will not.* A war raged within the fisherman.

At that moment the instinct to survive collided with his allegiance to Christ, and for just a moment allegiance won. Peter stood and stepped out of hiding and followed the noise till he saw the torch-lit jury in the courtyard of Caiaphas.

He stopped near a fire and warmed his hands. The fire sparked with irony. The night had been cold. The fire was hot. But Peter was neither. He was lukewarm.

"Peter followed at a distance" Luke described (22:54 NIV).

He was loyal . . . from a distance. That night he went close enough to see, but not close enough to be seen. The problem was, Peter was seen. Other people near the fire recognized him. "You were with him," they had challenged. "You were with the Nazarene." Three times people said it, and each time Peter denied it. And each time Jesus heard it.

Please understand that the main character in this drama of denial is not Peter, but Jesus. Jesus, who knows the hearts of all people, knew the denial of his friend. Three times the salt of Peter's betrayal stung the wounds of the Messiah.

How do I know Jesus knew? Because of what he did. "Then the Lord turned and looked straight at Peter" (Luke 22:61 NIV). When the rooster crowed, Jesus turned. His eyes searched for Peter and they found him. At that moment there were no soldiers, no accusers, no priests. At that predawn moment in Jerusalem there were only two people—Jesus and Peter.

Peter would never forget that look. Though Jesus' face was already bloody and bruised, his eyes were firm and focused. They were a scalpel, laying bare Peter's heart. Though the look had lasted only a moment, it lasted forever.

And now, days later on the Sea of Galilee, the look still seared. It wasn't the resurrection that occupied his thoughts. It wasn't the empty tomb. It wasn't the defeat of death. It was the eyes of Jesus seeing his failure. Peter knew them well. He'd seen them before. In fact he'd seen them on this very lake.

This wasn't the first night that Peter had spent on the Sea of Galilee. After all, he was a fisherman. He, like the others, worked at night. He knew the fish would feed near the surface during the cool of the night and return to the deep during the day. No, this wasn't the first night Peter had spent on the Sea of Galilee. Nor was it the first night he had caught nothing.

There was that time years before . . .

Most mornings Peter and his partners would sell their fish, repair their nets, and head home to rest with a bag of money and a feeling of satisfaction. This particular morning there was no money. There was no satisfaction. They had worked all through the night but had nothing to show for it except weary backs and worn nets.

And, what's worse, everyone knew it. Every morning the shore would become a market as the villagers came to buy their fish, but that day there were no fish.

Jesus was there that morning, teaching. As the people pressed there was little room for him to stand, so he asked Peter if his boat could be a platform. Peter agreed, maybe thinking the boat might as well be put to some good use.

Peter listens as Jesus teaches. It's good to hear something other than the slapping of waves. When Jesus finishes with the crowd, he turns to Peter. He has another request. He wants to go fishing. "Take the boat into deep water, and put your nets in the water to catch some fish" (Luke 5:4).

Peter groans. The last thing he wants to do is fish. The boat is clean. The nets are ready to dry. The sun is up and he is tired. It's time to go home. Besides, everyone is watching. They've already seen him come back empty-handed once. And, what's more, what does Jesus know about fishing?

So Peter speaks, "Master, we worked hard all night trying to catch fish" (v. 5).

Mark the weariness in the words.

"We worked hard." Scraping the hull. Carrying the nets. Pulling the oars. Throwing the nets high into the moonlit sky. Listening as they slap on the surface of the water.

"All night." The sky had gone from burnt orange to midnight black to morning gold. The hours had passed as slowly as the fleets of clouds before the moon. The fishermen's conversation had stilled and their shoulders ached. While the village slept, the men worked. All . . . night . . . long.

"Trying to catch fish." The night's events had been rhythmic: net swung and tossed high till it spread itself against the sky. Then wait. Let it sink. Pull it in. Do it again. Throw. Pull. Throw. Pull. Throw. Pull. Every toss had been a prayer. But every drag of the empty net had come back unanswered. Even the net sighed as the men pulled it out and prepared to throw it again.

For twelve hours they'd fished. And now . . . now Jesus is wanting to fish some more? And not just off the shore, but in the deep?

Peter sees his friends shrug their shoulders. He looks at the people on the beach watching him. He doesn't know what to do. Jesus may know a lot about a lot, but Peter knows about fishing. Peter knows when to work and when to quit. He knows there is a time to go on and a time to get out.

Common sense said it was time to get out. Logic said cut your losses and go home. Experience said pack it up and get some rest. But Jesus said, *"We can try again if you want."*

The most difficult journey is back to the place where you failed.

Jesus knows that. That's why he volunteers to go along. "The first outing was solo; this time I'll be with you. Try it again, this time with me on board."

And Peter reluctantly agrees to try again. "But you say to put the nets in the water, so I will" (Luke 5:5). It didn't make any sense, but he'd been around this Nazarene enough to know that his presence made a difference. That wedding in Cana? That sick child of the royal ruler? It's as if Jesus carried his own deck to the table.

So the oars dip again and the boat goes out. The anchor is set and the nets fly once more.

Peter watches as the net sinks, and he waits. He waits until the net spreads as far as his rope allows. The fishermen are quiet. Peter is quiet. Jesus is quiet. Suddenly the rope yanks. The net, heavy with fish, almost pulls Peter overboard.

"John, James!" he yells. "Come quick!"

Soon the boats are so full of fish that the port side rim dips close to the surface. Peter, ankle deep in flopping silver, turns to look at Jesus, only to find that Jesus is looking at him.

That's when he realizes who Jesus is.

What an odd place to meet God—on a fishing boat on a small sea in a remote country! But such is the practice of the God who comes into our world. Such is the encounter experienced by those who are willing to try again . . . with him.

Peter's life was never again the same after that catch.

He had turned his back on the sea to follow the Messiah. He had left the boats thinking he'd never return. But now he's back. Full circle. Same sea. Same boat. Maybe even the same spot.

But this isn't the same Peter. Three years of living with the Messiah have changed him. He's seen too much. Too many walking crippled, vacated graves, too many hours hearing his words. He's not the same Peter. It's the same Galilee, but a different fisherman.

Why did he return? What brought him back to Galilee after the crucifixion? Despair? Some think so—I don't. Hope dies hard for a man who has known Jesus. I think that's what Peter has. That's what brought him back. Hope. A bizarre hope that on the sea where he knew him first, he would know him again.

So Peter is in the boat, on the lake. Once again he's fished all night. Once again the sea has surrendered nothing.

His thoughts are interrupted by a shout from the shore. "Catch any fish?" Peter and John look up. Probably a villager. "No!" they yell. "Try the other side!" the voice yells back. John looks at Peter. What harm? So out sails the net. Peter wraps the rope around his wrist to wait.

But there is no wait. The rope pulls taut and the net catches. Peter sets his weight against the side of the boat and begins to bring in the net; reaching down, pulling up, reaching down, pulling up. He's so intense with the task, he misses the message.

John doesn't. The moment is déjà vu. This has happened before. The long night. The empty net. The call to cast again. Fish flapping on the floor of the boat. Wait a minute. He lifts his eyes to the man on the shore. "It's him," he whispers.

Then louder, "It's Jesus."

Then shouting,"It's the Lord, Peter. It's the Lord!"

Peter turns and looks. Jesus has come. Not just Jesus the teacher, but Jesus the death-defeater, Jesus the king . . . Jesus the victor over darkness. Jesus the God of heaven and earth is on the shore . . . and he's building a fire.

Peter plunges into the water, swims to the shore, and stumbles out wet and shivering and stands in front of the friend he betrayed. Jesus has prepared a bed of coals. Both are aware of the last time Peter had stood near a fire. Peter had failed God, but God had come to him.

For one of the few times in his life, Peter is silent. What words would suffice? The moment is too holy for words. God is offering breakfast to the friend who betrayed him. And Peter is once again finding grace at Galilee.

What do you say at a moment like this?

What do *you* say at a moment such as this?

It's just you and God. You and God both know what you did. And neither one of you is proud of it. What do you do?

You might consider doing what Peter did. Stand in God's presence. Stand in his sight. Stand still and wait. Sometimes that's all a soul can do. Too repentant to speak, but too hopeful to leave—we just stand.

Stand amazed.
He has come back.
He invites you to try again. This time, with him.

15

THE TENDERNESS OF GOD

*When You Wonder If
God Cares*

Two days later there was a wedding in the town of Cana in Galilee. Jesus' mother was there, and Jesus and his followers were also invited to the wedding. When all the wine was gone, Jesus' mother said to him, "They have no more wine."

Jesus answered, "Dear woman, why come to me? My time has not yet come."

His mother said to the servants, "Do whatever he tells you to do."

In that place there were six stone water jars that the Jews used in their washing ceremony. Each jar held about twenty or thirty gallons.

Jesus said to the servants, "Fill the jars with water." So they filled the jars to the top.

Then he said to them, "Now take some out and give it to the master of the feast."

So they took the water to the master. When he tasted it, the water had become wine. He did not know where the wine came from, but the servants who had brought the water knew. The master of the wedding called the bridegroom and said to him, "People always serve the best wine first. Later, after the guests have been drinking awhile, they serve the cheaper wine. But you have saved the best wine till now."

So in Cana of Galilee Jesus did his first miracle. There he showed his glory, and his followers believed in him.

John 2:1–11

> "People always serve the best wine
> first. Later, after the guests have been
> drinking awhile, they serve the
> cheaper wine. But you have saved the
> best wine till now."
>
> John 2:10

Let's pretend you are an angel. (That may be a stretch for some of you, but let's give it a try.)

You are an angel in the era before the Messiah. God has not yet come to the earth, but he soon will and that's where you come in. You receive notice that you've been given a special assignment. A once-in-an-eternity opportunity. You've been asked to serve on a special committee. Quite an honor, don't you think?

Michael chairs the heavenly task force. "Let's begin by choosing the first miracle," he states. "The first miracle is crucial. It's the lead-off proclamation. It's the vanguard demonstration. It must be chosen carefully."

"Must be powerful," someone volunteers.

"Undeniable."

"Unforgettable," chimes a third.

"We are in agreement, then," affirms Michael. "The first miracle of God on earth must have clout. Any ideas?"

Angelic creativity begins to whir.

"Have him raise a person from the dead."

"Or a whole cemetery from the dead!"

"Yeah, vacate the place."

"What about feeding every hungry person one meal?"

"Too easy. How about removing all the disease from the planet?"

"Bingo. I like that idea."

"I know," the voice is yours. All the other angels turn to look at you. "What if he rids the earth of all evil? I mean, with one great swoop all the bad is gone and just the good remains."

The group is silent. "Not bad," says one.

"Good thinking," says another.

"Get it done once and for all," agrees Michael. "It's settled. The first miracle will obliterate evil from the earth!"

Wings rustle with approval and you smile with pride. (You may get a promotion out of this.)

"Now let's move on to the second miracle . . ."

Sound far-fetched? Maybe, but the story is not without a couple of threads of truth.

One is that Jesus did have a plan. You can tell by some phrases he uses.

> "The right time for me has not yet come" (John 7:6).
> "The time has come for the Son of Man to receive his glory" (John 12:23).
> "The chosen time is near" (Matt. 26:18).
> "The time has come for the Son of Man to be handed over to sinful people" (Mark 14:41).
> "He looked toward heaven and prayed, 'Father, the time has come . . .'" (John 17:1).

Look at those words. "The right time has not yet come." "The time has come." "The chosen time." "The time has come." What do those phrases imply? A schedule. They represent a definite order of events. The mission of Christ was planned. I doubt if a committee ever existed, but a plan did.

There is a second shred of truth in my little scenario. Not only was there a plan in Christ's ministry, there was also a first miracle. What was it?

The plot is almost too simple. Jesus and his disciples are at a wedding. The host runs out of wine. All the stores are closed, so Jesus, at his mother's urging, transforms six jugs of water into six jugs of wine.

That's it. That's the lead-off hitter. Pretty low key, don't you think? Certainly doesn't have the punch of calling a person from the dead or the flair of straightening a crippled leg.

Or does it? Maybe there is more to this than we think.

You see, a wedding in the day of Christ was no small event. It usually began with a sundown ceremony at the synagogue. People would then leave the synagogue and begin a long, candlelight procession through the city, winding their way through the soft evening sunlight of the city streets. The couple would be escorted past as many homes as possible so everyone could wish them well. After the processional, however, the couple didn't go on a honeymoon; the honeymoon was brought to them.

They would go home to a party. For several days there would be gift-giving, speechmaking, food-eating and—you guessed it!—wine-drinking. Food and wine were taken very seriously. The host honored the guests by keeping their plates full and their cups overflowing. It was considered an insult to the guests if the host ran out of food or wine.

Hospitality at a wedding was a sacred duty. So serious were these social customs that, if they were not observed, lawsuits could be brought by the injured parties!

"Without wine," said the rabbis, "there is no joy." Wine was crucial, not for drunkenness, which was considered a disgrace, but for what it demonstrated. The presence of wine stated that this was a special day and that all the guests were special guests.

The absence of wine, then, was a social embarrassment.

Mary, the mother of Jesus, is one of the first to notice that the wine has run out. She goes to her son and points out the problem: "They have no more wine."

Jesus' response? "Dear woman, why come to me? My time has not yet come" (v. 4).

There are those words again. "My time." Jesus is aware of the plan. He has a place and a time for his first miracle. And this isn't it.

About now the angelic committee on the miracles of the Messiah lets out a collective sigh of relief.

"Whew, for a minute there, I thought he was going to blow it."

"Me, too. Can you imagine Jesus inaugurating his ministry with a water-to-wine miracle?"

"That's it, Jesus, say no. Stick to the plan."

Jesus knows the plan. At first, it appears he is going to stay with it. But as he hears his mother and looks into the faces of the wedding party, he reconsiders. The significance of the plan is slowly eclipsed by his concern for the people. Timing is important, but people are more so.

As a result, he changes his plan to meet the needs of some friends. Incredible. The schedule of heaven is altered so some friends won't be embarrassed. The inaugural miracle is motivated—not by tragedy or famine or moral collapse—but by concern for friends who are in a bind.

Now if you're an angel on the committee of Messianic miracles, you don't like that one bit. No, sir. You don't like this move on the part of Jesus. Everything about it is wrong. Wrong time. Wrong place. Wrong miracle.

"Come on, Jesus. Remember the schedule," you urge. "Remember the strategy. This isn't the way we had it planned."

No, if you're an angel on the committee, you don't like this move.

But if you're a human who has ever been embarrassed, you like this very much. Why? Because this miracle tells you that what matters to you matters to God.

You probably think that's true when it comes to the big stuff. When it comes to the major-league difficulties like death, disease, sin, and disaster—you know that God cares.

But what about the smaller things? What about grouchy bosses or flat tires or lost dogs? What about broken dishes, late flights, toothaches, or a crashed hard disk? Do these matter to God?

I mean, he's got a universe to run. He's got the planets to keep balanced and presidents and kings to watch over. He's got wars to worry with and famines to fix. Who am I to tell him about my ingrown toenail?

I'm glad you asked. Let me tell you who you are. In fact, let me *proclaim* who you are.

> You are an heir of God and a co-heir with Christ (Rom. 8:17).
>
> You are eternal, like an angel (Luke 20:36).
>
> You have a crown that will last forever (1 Cor. 9:25).
>
> You are a holy priest (1 Pet. 2:5), a treasured possession (Exod. 19:5).
>
> You were chosen before the creation of the world (Eph. 1:4). You are destined for "praise, fame, and honor, and you will be a holy people to the LORD your God" (Deut. 26:19).

But more than any of the above—more significant than any title or position—is the simple fact that you are God's child. "The Father has loved us so much that we are called children of God. And we really are his children" (1 John 3:1).

I love that last phrase! "We really are his children." It's as if John knew some of us would shake our heads and say, "Naw, not me. Mother Teresa, maybe. Billy Graham, all right. But not me." If those are your feelings, John added that phrase for you.

"We *really* are his children."

As a result, if something is important to you, it's important to God.

If you are a parent you know that. Imagine if you noticed an infected sore on the hand of your five-year-old son. You ask him what's wrong, and he says that he has a splinter. You ask him when it happened. He says last week! You ask him why he didn't tell you, and he says, "I didn't want to bother you. I knew you had all those things to do running the household and all, I didn't want to get in your way."

"Get in my way? Get in my way! I'm your dad. You're my son. My job is to help. I hurt when you hurt."

I have a perfect example of this on videotape. My eight-year-old daughter Jenna sang a solo at an appreciation banquet.

I agreed to stay home with our other two daughters if my wife would film the performance. When they came home, they had quite a story to tell and quite a tape to show.

Jenna forgot her lines. As she stood onstage in front of a large audience, her mind went blank. Since Denalyn was filming the moment, I saw the crisis through her eyes, the eyes of a mom. You can tell Denalyn is getting nervous the minute Jenna is getting forgetful—the camera begins to shake. "It's OK, it's OK," Denalyn's voice assures. She begins singing the words so Jenna will remember. But it's too late. Jenna says "I'm sorry" to the audience, bursts into tears, and bolts off the stage.

At this point Mom drops the camera and runs after Jenna. The camera records the floor and Denalyn's voice saying, "Come here, honey."

Why did Denalyn do that? Why did she drop everything and run after her daughter? (By the way, Jenna recovered. Denalyn dried her tears. The two rehearsed the lyrics. And Jenna sang and received a loud ovation.)

Now, why did Denalyn go to all that trouble? In the great scheme of things, does a social embarrassment matter that much? You know the answer before I tell you. To an eight-year-old girl, it's crucial. And because it was important to Jenna, it was important to Mom.

And because you are God's child, if it's important to you, it's important to God.

Why did Jesus change the water to wine? To impress the crowd? No, they didn't even know he did it. To get the wedding master's attention? No, he thought the groom was being generous. Why did Jesus do it? What motivated his first miracle?

His friends were embarrassed. What bothered them bothered him. If it hurts the child, it hurts the father.

So go ahead. Tell God what hurts. Talk to him. He won't turn you away. He won't think it's silly. "For our high priest is *able to understand* our weaknesses. When he lived on earth, he was tempted in every way that we are, but he did not sin. Let us, then, feel very sure that we can come before God's throne where there is grace" (Heb. 4:15–16, emphasis added).

Does God care about the little things in our lives? You better believe it.

If it matters to you, it matters to him.

16

THE MADMAN TURNED MISSIONARY

When You Encounter Evil

Jesus and his followers went to the other side of the lake to the area of the Gerasene people. When Jesus got out of the boat, instantly a man with an evil spirit came to him from the burial caves. This man lived in the caves, and no one could tie him up, not even with a chain. Many times people had used chains to tie the man's hands and feet, but he always broke them off. No one was strong enough to control him. Day and night he would wander around the burial caves and on the hills, screaming and cutting himself with stones. While Jesus was still far away, the man saw him, ran to him, and fell down before him.

The man shouted in a loud voice, "What do you want with me, Jesus, Son of the Most High God? I command you in God's name not to torture me!" He said this because Jesus was saying to him, "You evil spirit, come out of the man."

Then Jesus asked him, "What is your name?"

He answered, "My name is Legion, because we are many spirits."

He begged Jesus again and again not to send them out of that area.

A large herd of pigs was feeding on a hill near there. The demons begged Jesus, "Send us into the pigs; let us go into them." So Jesus allowed them to do this. The evil spirits left the man and went into the pigs. Then the herd of pigs—about two thousand of them—rushed down the hill into the lake and were drowned.

The herdsmen ran away and went to the town and to the countryside, telling everyone about this. So people went out to see what had happened. They came to Jesus and saw the man who used to have the many evil spirits, sitting, clothed, and in his right mind. And they were frightened. The people who saw this told the others what had happened to the man who had the demons living in him, and they told about the pigs. Then the people began to beg Jesus to leave their area.

As Jesus was getting back into the boat, the man who was freed from the demons begged to go with him.

But Jesus would not let him. He said, "Go home to your family and tell them how much the Lord has done for you and how he has had mercy on you." So the man left and began to tell the people in the Ten Towns about what Jesus had done for him. And everyone was amazed.

Mark 5:1–20

> They came to Jesus and saw the man
> who used to have the many evil
> spirits, sitting, clothed, and in his right
> mind.
>
> Mark 5:15

---

*H*ere's a question for you trivia hounds. Who was the first missionary Jesus ever sent?

Someone well trained, right? Someone with an intimate relationship with Christ. A devoted follower. A close disciple. One with a thorough knowledge of Scripture and sacrifice, wouldn't you think?

Let me give you a hint. To find him don't go to the Great Commission. Don't turn to the names of the apostles. This vanguard spokesman was not on that list.

How about the seventy-two disciples sent out by Christ? Sorry, wrong again. The epistles? No. Long before Paul picked up a pen, this preacher was already at work.

Where did Jesus go to find his first missionary? (You won't believe this.) A cemetery.

Who was the first ambassador he commissioned? (You're not going to buy this either.) A lunatic. The man Jesus sent out was a madman turned missionary. His story is found in the fifth chapter of Mark's Gospel.

> When Jesus got out of the boat, instantly a man with an evil
> spirit came to him from the burial caves. This man lived in
> the caves, and no one could tie him up, not even with a
> chain. Many times people had used chains to tie the man's

hands and feet, but he always broke them off. No one was strong enough to control him. Day and night he would wander around the burial caves and on the hills, screaming and cutting himself with stones.

Mark 5:2–5

He's the man your mom told you to avoid. He's the fellow the police routinely lock up. He's the deranged man who stalks neighborhoods and murders families. This is the face that fills the screen during the evening news.

And this is the first missionary of the church.

Palestine didn't know what to do with him. They restrained him, but he broke the chains. He ripped off his clothes. He lived in caves. He cut himself with rocks. He was a rabid coyote on the loose, a menace to society. Of absolutely no good to anyone. No one had a place for him—except Jesus.

Even today the best that modern medicine could offer such a man is medication and extensive treatment. Maybe, with much time, expense, and professional help, such destructive behavior could be curtailed. But it would take years.

With Jesus it takes seconds.

The encounter is explosive. The disciples' boat beaches near a graveyard and a herd of pigs. Both are ritually and culturally unclean for Jews. As Jesus steps out, a crazy man storms out of a cavern.

Wild hair. Bloody wrists. Scratched skin. Fury encased in flesh. Naked bedlam. Arms flailing and voice screaming. The apostles gawk and gulp and put a foot back in the boat.

They are horrified. But Jesus isn't. Read the next few verses carefully, for they provide a rare privilege—a glimpse into the unseen warfare. For just a few minutes the invisible conflict becomes visible and we are offered a position overlooking the battlefield.

Jesus speaks first: "You evil spirit, come out of the man" (v. 8).

157

The spirit panics: "What do you want with me, Jesus, Son of the Most High God?" (v. 7).

Jesus wants the man back. The demons muster no challenge. They offer no threat. They've heard this voice before. When God demands, the demons have one response. They plead. They "begged Jesus again and again not to send them out of that area" (v. 10).

Jesus' mere appearance humbles the demons. Though they had dominated this man, they cower before God. Though they had laced a region with fear, they beg for mercy from Jesus. His words reduce them to sniveling, groveling weaklings.

Feeling safer in a herd of pigs than in the presence of God, the demons ask to be sent into the swine. Jesus consents, and two thousand possessed pigs hurl themselves into the sea.

And all the while the disciples do nothing. While Jesus fights, the followers stare. They don't know anything else to do.

Can you relate? Are you watching a world out of control and don't know what to do? If so, do what the disciples did: When the fighting is fierce, stand back and let the Father fight.

I have a picture in my mental scrapbook that illustrates this principle. In the scene, my father and I are battling a storm in a fishing boat. We are surrounded by a mountain range of white tops, most taller than either of us. The coastline is hidden, the fog is thickening, and we are honestly beginning to wonder if we will make it back to shore.

I am young, maybe nine. The boat is small, perhaps ten feet. And the waves are high, high enough to overturn our craft. The sky rumbles, the clouds billow, and the lightning zigzags.

Dad has directed the boat toward the nearest beach, taking us bow first into the waves. He sits in the rear with a hand on the throttle and his face into the wind. I sit in the front looking back toward him. Rain stings my bare neck and soaks my shirt. One wave after another picks us up and slaps us down. I grab both sides of the boat and hang on.

In vain I search for the coast. It's buried by fog. I look for the sun . . . it's hidden by the clouds. I look for other boats . . . I see only waves. Everything I see frightens me. There is only one reassuring sight, the face of my father. Rain-splattered and grimacing, he peers into the storm. Water drips off the bill of his baseball cap, and his shirt is stuck to his skin.

Right then I made a decision. I quit looking at the storm and watched only my father. It just made sense. Watching the waves brought fear; watching my father brought calm. So I focused on Dad. So intent was my gaze that three decades later I can still see him guiding us out of the billows.

God wants us to do the same. He wants us to focus our eyes on him. What good does it do to focus on the storm? Why study the enemy? We won't defeat him. Only God will. The disciples can't destroy Satan; only God can.

And that's what Jesus did.

As the stunned disciples look on, Jesus goes into action and God delivers a lunatic. Pigs are embodied by demons. And a disciple is made in a cemetery.

Outlandish story? Just wait. It's not over yet. If you think the reaction of the demons is bizarre, wait until you see the response of the people.

The pig herders ran to the city and told everyone what they had seen.

So the people went out to see for themselves.

> They came to Jesus and saw the man who used to have the many evil spirits, sitting, clothed, and in his right mind. And they were frightened. The people who saw this told the others what had happened to the man who had the demons living in him, and they told about the pigs. Then the people began to beg Jesus to leave their area.
>
> Mark 5:15–17

They did what? *The people began to beg Jesus to leave the area*.

You mean the people asked Jesus to leave? That's right. Rather than thank him, they dismissed him? You got it. What would cause people to do such a thing?

Good question. What would cause people to prefer pigs and lunatics over the presence of God?

Or better . . .

What would cause an alcoholic to prefer drunken misery over sobriety?

What would cause a church to prefer slumber over revival?

What would cause a nation to prefer slavery over freedom?

What would cause people to prefer yesterday's traditions over today's living God?

The answer? Fear of change. Change is hard work. It's easier to follow the same old path than to move out into uncharted territory.

So the people dismissed Jesus. And since Jesus never goes where he isn't invited, he steps back into the boat.

Now watch what happens next.

> As Jesus was getting back into the boat, the man who was freed from the demons begged to go with him.
> But Jesus would not let him.
>
> Mark 5:18

Strange way to treat a new believer, don't you think? Why wouldn't Jesus take him along? Simple. He had greater plans for him. "Go home to your family and tell them how much the Lord has done for you and how he has had mercy on you" (v. 19).

There it is. The commissioning of the first missionary. One minute insane, the next in Christ. No training. No teaching. All he knew was that Jesus could scare the hell out of hell and apparently that was enough.

But even more surprising than the man who was sent is the fact that *anyone* was sent. I wouldn't have sent a missionary to some people who had just given me the boot, would you? A plague perhaps, but not a missionary. But Christ did.

And Christ does. He still sends the message to the unworthy. And he still uses the unworthy as messengers.

After all, look who's reading this book.

And look who wrote it.

17

SEEING THE UNSEEN

---

*When You Are Afraid
of the Future*

When Jesus went in the boat back to the other side of the lake, a large crowd gathered around him there. A leader of the synagogue, named Jairus, came there, saw Jesus, and fell at his feet. He begged Jesus, saying again and again, "My daughter is dying. Please come and put your hands on her so she will be healed and will live." So Jesus went with him. . . .

While Jesus was still speaking, some people came from the house of the synagogue leader. They said, "Your daughter is dead. There is no need to bother the teacher anymore."

But Jesus paid no attention to what they said. He told the synagogue leader, "Don't be afraid; just believe."

Jesus let only Peter, James, and John the brother of James go with him. When they came to the house of the synagogue leader, Jesus found many people there making lots of noise and crying loudly. Jesus entered the house and said to them, "Why are you crying and making so much noise? The child is not dead, only asleep." But they laughed at him. So, after throwing them out of the house, Jesus took the child's father and mother and his three followers into the room where the child was. Taking hold of the girl's hand, he said to her, "Talitha, koum!" (This means, "Young girl, I tell you to stand up!") At once the girl stood right up and began walking. (She was twelve years old.) Everyone was completely amazed. Jesus gave them strict orders not to tell people about this. Then he told them to give the girl something to eat.

Mark 5:21–24, 35–43

Faith means . . . knowing that something is real even if we do not see it.

Hebrews 11:1

Last night I tried to teach my daughters to see with their eyes closed.

I asked Jenna, the eight-year-old, to go to one side of the den. I had Andrea, the six-year-old, stand on the other. Three-year-old Sara and I sat on the couch in the middle and watched. Jenna's job was to close her eyes and walk. Andrea's job was to be Jenna's eyes and talk her safely across the room.

With phrases like, "Take two baby steps to the left" and "Take four giant steps straight ahead," Andrea successfully navigated her sister through a treacherous maze of chairs, a vacuum cleaner, and a laundry basket.

Then Jenna took her turn. She guided Andrea past her mom's favorite lamp and shouted just in time to keep her from colliding into the wall when she thought her right foot was her left foot.

After several treks through the darkness, they stopped and we processed.

"I didn't like it," Jenna complained. "It's scary going where you can't see."

"I was afraid I was going to fall," Andrea agreed. "I kept taking little steps to be safe."

I can relate, can't you? We grownups don't like the dark either. But we walk in it. We, like Jenna, often complain about how scary it is to walk where we can't see. And we, like Andrea, often take timid steps so we won't fall.

We've reason to be cautious: We are blind. We can't see the future. We have absolutely no vision beyond the present. I can't tell you with certainty that I will live long enough to finish this paragraph. (Whew, I did!) Nor can you tell me you'll live long enough to read the next one. (Hope you do!)

I'm not talking nearsightedness or obstructed view; I'm talking opaque blindness. I'm not talking about a condition that passes with childhood; I'm describing a condition that passes only with death. We are blind. Blind to the future.

It's one limitation we all share. The wealthy are just as blind as the poor. The educated are just as sightless as the unschooled. And the famous know as little about the future as the unknown.

None of us know how our children will turn out. None of us know the day we will die. No one knows whom he or she will marry or even if marriage lies before him or her. We are universally, absolutely, unalterably blind.

We are all Jenna with her eyes shut, groping through a dark room, listening for a familiar voice—but with one difference. Her surroundings are familiar and friendly. Ours can be hostile and fatal. Her worst fear is a stubbed toe. Our worst fear is more threatening: cancer, divorce, loneliness, death.

And try as we might to walk as straight as we can, chances are a toe is going to get stubbed and we are going to get hurt.

Just ask Jairus. He is a man who has tried to walk as straight as he can. But Jairus was a man whose path has taken a sudden turn into a cave—a dark cave. And he doesn't want to enter it alone.

Jairus is the leader of the synagogue. That may not mean much to you and me, but in the days of Christ the leader of the synagogue was the most important man in the community. The synagogue was the center of religion, education, leadership, and social activity. The leader of the synagogue was the senior religious leader, the highest-ranking professor, the mayor, and the best-known citizen all in one.

Jairus has it all. Job security. A guaranteed welcome at the coffee shop. A pension plan. Golf every Thursday and an annual all-expenses-paid trip to the national convention.

Who could ask for more? Yet Jairus does. He *has* to ask for more. In fact, he would trade the whole package of perks and privileges for just one assurance—that his daughter will live.

The Jairus we see in this story is not the clear-sighted, black-frocked, nicely groomed civic leader. He is instead a blind man begging for a gift. He fell at Jesus' feet, "saying again and again, 'My daughter is dying. Please come and put your hands on her so she will be healed and will live'" (Mark 5:23).

He doesn't barter with Jesus. ("You do me a favor, and I'll see you are taken care of for life.") He doesn't negotiate with Jesus. ("The guys in Jerusalem are getting pretty testy about your antics. Tell you what, you handle this problem of mine, and I'll make a few calls . . .") He doesn't make excuses. ("Normally, I'm not this desperate, Jesus, but I've got a small problem.")

He just pleads.

There are times in life when everything you have to offer is nothing compared to what you are asking to receive. Jairus is at such a point. What could a man offer in exchange for his child's life? So there are no games. No haggling. No masquerades. The situation is starkly simple: Jairus is blind to the future and Jesus knows the future. So Jairus asks for his help.

And Jesus, who loves the honest heart, goes to give it.

And God, who knows what it is like to lose a child, empowers his son.

But before Jesus and Jairus get very far, they are interrupted by emissaries from his house.

"Your daughter is dead. There is no need to bother the teacher anymore" (v. 35).

Get ready. Hang on to your hat. Here's where the story gets moving. Jesus goes from being led to leading, from being convinced by Jairus to *convincing* Jairus. From being admired to being laughed at, from helping out the people to casting out the people.

Here is where Jesus takes control.

"But Jesus paid no attention to what they said . . ." (v. 36).

I love that line! It describes the critical principle for seeing the unseen: Ignore what people say. Block them out. Turn them off. Close your ears. And, if you have to, walk away.

Ignore the ones who say it's too late to start over.

Disregard those who say you'll never amount to anything.

Turn a deaf ear toward those who say that you aren't smart enough, fast enough, tall enough, or big enough—ignore them.

Faith sometimes begins by stuffing your ears with cotton.

Jesus turns immediately to Jairus and pleads: "Don't be afraid; just believe" (v. 36).

Jesus compels Jairus to see the unseen. When Jesus says, "Just believe . . . ," he is imploring, "Don't limit your possibilities to the visible. Don't listen only for the audible. Don't be controlled by the logical. Believe there is more to life than meets the eye!"

"Trust me," Jesus is pleading. "Don't be afraid; just trust."

A father in the Bahamas cried out the same plea to his young son who was trapped in a burning house. The two-story structure was engulfed in flames, and the family—the father, mother, and several children—was on its way out when the smallest boy became terrified and ran back upstairs. His father, outside, shouted to him: "Jump, son, jump! I'll catch you." The boy cried: "But Daddy, I can't see you." "I know," his father called, "but I can see you."

The father could see, even though the son could not.

A similar example of faith was found on the wall of a concentration camp. On it a prisoner had carved the words:

> I believe in the sun, even though it doesn't shine,
> I believe in love, even when it isn't shown,
> I believe in God, even when he doesn't speak.

I try to imagine the person who etched those words. I try to envision his skeletal hand gripping the broken glass or stone that cut into the wall. I try to imagine his eyes squinting through the darkness as he carved each letter. What hand could have cut such a conviction? What eyes could have seen good in such horror?

There is only one answer: Eyes that chose to see the unseen.

As Paul wrote: "We set our eyes not on what we see but on what we cannot see. What we see will last only a short time, but what we cannot see will last forever" (2 Cor. 4:18).

Jesus is asking Jairus to see the unseen. To make a choice. Either to live by the facts or to see by faith. When tragedy strikes we, too, are left to choose what we see. We can see either the hurt or the Healer.

The choice is ours.

Jairus made his choice. He opted for faith and Jesus . . . and faith *in* Jesus led him to his daughter.

At the house Jesus and Jairus encounter a group of mourners. Jesus is troubled by their wailing. It bothers him that they express such anxiety over death. "Why are you crying and making so much noise? The child is not dead, only asleep" (v. 39).

That's not a rhetorical question. It's an honest one. From his perspective, the girl is not dead—she is only asleep. From God's viewpoint, death is not permanent. It is a necessary step for passing from this world to the next. It's not an end; it's a beginning.

As a young boy I had two great loves—playing and eating. Summers were made for afternoons on the baseball diamond and meals at Mom's dinner table. Mom had a rule, however. Dirty, sweaty boys could never eat at the table. Her first words to us as we came home were always, "Go clean up and take off those clothes if you want to eat."

Now no boy is fond of bathing and dressing, but I never once complained and defied my mom by saying, "I'd rather stink than eat!" In my economy a bath and a clean shirt were a small price to pay for a good meal.

And from God's perspective death is a small price to pay for the privilege of sitting at his table. "Flesh and blood cannot have a part in the kingdom of God. . . . This body that can be destroyed *must* clothe itself with something that can never be destroyed. And this body that dies *must* clothe itself with something that can never die" (1 Cor. 15:50, 53, emphasis added).

God is even more insistent than my mom was. In order to sit at his table, a change of clothing *must* occur. And we must die in order for our body to be exchanged for a new one. So, from God's viewpoint, death is not to be dreaded; it is to be welcomed.

And when he sees people crying and mourning over death, he wants to know, "Why are you crying?" (v. 39).

When we see death, we see disaster. When Jesus sees death, he sees deliverance.

That's too much for the people to take. "They laughed at him" (v. 40). (The next time people mock you, you might remember they mocked him, too.)

Now look closely because you aren't going to believe what Jesus does next. He throws the mourners out! That's what the text says, "after throwing them out of the house . . ." (v. 40). He doesn't just ask them to leave. He *throws* them out. He picks them up by collar and belt and sets them sailing. Jesus' response was decisive and strong. In the original text, the word used here is the same word used to describe what Jesus did to the moneychangers in the temple. It's the same verb used *thirty-eight* times to describe what Jesus did to the demons.

Why? Why such force? Why such intolerance?

Perhaps the answer is found by going back to last evening's living-room experience. After Jenna and Andrea had taken turns guiding each other through the den, I decided to add a diabolical twist. On the last trip, I snuck up behind Jenna, who was walking with her eyes shut, and began whispering, "Don't listen to her. Listen to me. I'll take care of you."

Jenna stopped. She analyzed the situation and made her choice between the two voices. "Be quiet, Daddy," she giggled and then continued in Andrea's direction.

Undeterred, I grabbed the lid of a pan, held it next to her ear, and banged it with a spoon. She jumped and stopped, startled by the noise. Andrea, seeing that her pilgrim was frightened, did a great thing. She ran across the room and threw her arms around her sister and said, "Don't worry, I'm right here."

She wasn't about to let the noise distract Jenna from the journey.

And God isn't going to let the noise distract you from yours. He's still busy casting out the critics and silencing the voices that could deter you.

Some of his work you have seen. Most of it you haven't. Only when you get home will you know how many times he has protected you from luring voices. Only eternity will reveal the time he:

> Interfered with the transfer, protecting you from involvement in unethical business.
>
> Fogged in the airport, distancing you from a shady opportunity.
>
> Flattened your tire, preventing you from checking into the hotel and meeting a seductive man.

And only heaven will show the times he protected you by:

> Giving you a mate who loves God more than you do.
>
> Opening the door for a new business so you could attend the same church.
>
> Having the right voice with the right message on the right radio station the day you needed his encouragement.

Mark it down: God knows you and I are blind. He knows living by faith and not by sight doesn't come naturally. And I think that's one reason he raised Jairus's daughter from the dead. Not for her sake—she was better off in heaven. But for our sake—to teach us that heaven sees when we trust.

One final thought from the seeing-with-your-eyes-closed experiment. I asked Jenna how she could hear Andrea's voice guiding her across the room when I was trying to distract her by whispering in her ear.

Her answer? "I just concentrated and listened as hard as I could."

18

JOSEPH'S PRAYER

---

*When You're Confused by
God's Actions*

Joseph . . . did what the Lord's
angel had told him to do.

Matthew 1:24

$\mathcal{T}$he white space between Bible verses is fertile soil for questions. One can hardly read Scripture without whispering, "I wonder . . ."

"I wonder if Eve ever ate any more fruit."

"I wonder if Noah slept well during storms."

"I wonder if Jonah liked fish or if Jeremiah had friends."

"Did Moses avoid bushes? Did Jesus tell jokes? Did Peter ever try water-walking again?"

"Would any woman have married Paul had he asked?"

The Bible is a fence full of knotholes through which we can peek but not see the whole picture. It's a scrapbook of snapshots capturing people in encounters with God, but not always recording the result. So we wonder:

When the woman caught in adultery went home, what did she say to her husband?

After the demoniac was delivered, what did he do for a living?

After Jairus's daughter was raised from the dead, did she ever regret it?

Knotholes and snapshots and "I wonders." You'll find them in every chapter about every person. But nothing stirs so many questions as does the birth of Christ. Characters appear and disappear before we can ask them anything. The innkeeper too busy to welcome God—did he ever learn who he turned away? The shepherds—did they ever hum the song the angels sang? The wise men who followed the star—what was it like to worship a toddler? And Joseph, especially Joseph. I've got questions for Joseph.

> Did you and Jesus arm wrestle? Did he ever let you win?
>
> Did you ever look up from your prayers and see Jesus listening?
>
> How do you say "Jesus" in Egyptian?
>
> What ever happened to the wise men?
>
> What ever happened to you?

We don't know what happened to Joseph. His role in Act I is so crucial that we expect to see him the rest of the drama—but with the exception of a short scene with twelve-year-old Jesus in Jerusalem, he never reappears. The rest of his life is left to speculation, and we are left with our questions.

But of all my questions, my first would be about Bethlehem. I'd like to know about the night in the stable. I can picture Joseph there. Moonlit pastures. Stars twinkle above. Bethlehem sparkles in the distance. There he is, pacing outside the stable.

What was he thinking while Jesus was being born? What was on his mind while Mary was giving birth? He'd done all he could do—heated the water, prepared a place for Mary to lie. He'd made Mary as comfortable as she could be in a barn and then he stepped out. She'd asked to be alone, and Joseph has never felt more so.

In that eternity between his wife's dismissal and Jesus' arrival, what was he thinking? He walked into the night and looked into the stars. Did he pray?

For some reason, I don't see him silent; I see Joseph animated, pacing. Head shaking one minute, fist shaking the next. This isn't what he had in mind. I wonder what he said . . .

This isn't the way I planned it, God. Not at all. My child being born in a stable? This isn't the way I thought it would be.

A cave with sheep and donkeys, hay and straw? My wife giving birth with only the stars to hear her pain?

This isn't at all what I imagined. No, I imagined family. I imagined grandmothers. I imagined neighbors clustered outside the door and friends standing at my side. I imagined the house erupting with the first cry of the infant. Slaps on the back. Loud laughter. Jubilation.

That's how I thought it would be.

The midwife would hand me my child and all the people would applaud. Mary would rest and we would celebrate. All of Nazareth would celebrate.

But now. Now look. Nazareth is five days' journey away. And here we are in a . . . in a sheep pasture. Who will celebrate with us? The sheep? The shepherds? The stars?

This doesn't seem right. What kind of husband am I? I provide no midwife to aid my wife. No bed to rest her back. Her pillow is a blanket from my donkey. My house for her is a shed of hay and straw.

The smell is bad, the animals are loud. Why, I even smell like a shepherd myself.

Did I miss something? Did I, God?

When you sent the angel and spoke of the son being born—this isn't what I pictured. I envisioned Jerusalem, the temple, the priests, and the people gathered to watch. A pageant perhaps. A parade. A banquet at least. I mean, this is the Messiah!

Or, if not born in Jerusalem, how about Nazareth? Wouldn't Nazareth have been better? At least there I have my house and my business. Out here, what do I have? A weary mule, a stack of firewood, and a pot of warm water. This is not the way I wanted it to be! This is not the way I wanted my son.

Oh my, I did it again. I did it again didn't I, Father? I don't mean to do that; it's just that I forget. He's not my son . . . he's yours.

The child is yours. The plan is yours. The idea is yours. And forgive me for asking but . . . is this how God enters the world?

The coming of the angel, I've accepted. The questions people asked about the pregnancy, I can tolerate. The trip to Bethlehem, fine. But why a birth in a stable, God?

Any minute now Mary will give birth. Not to a child, but to the Messiah. Not to an infant, but to God. That's what the angel said. That's what Mary believes. And, God, my God, that's what I want to believe. But surely you can understand; it's not easy. It seems so . . . so . . . so . . . bizarre.

I'm unaccustomed to such strangeness, God. I'm a carpenter. I make things fit. I square off the edges. I follow the plumb line. I measure twice before I cut once. Surprises are not the friend of a builder. I like to know the plan. I like to see the plan before I begin.

But this time I'm not the builder, am I? This time I'm a tool. A hammer in your grip. A nail between your fingers. A chisel in your hands. This project is yours, not mine.

I guess it's foolish of me to question you. Forgive my struggling. Trust doesn't come easy to me, God. But you never said it would be easy, did you?

One final thing, Father. The angel you sent? Any chance you could send another? If not an angel, maybe a person? I don't know anyone around here and some company would be nice. Maybe the innkeeper or a traveler? Even a shepherd would do.

I wonder. Did Joseph ever pray such a prayer? Perhaps he did. Perhaps he didn't.

But you probably have.

You've stood where Joseph stood. Caught between what God says and what makes sense. You've done what he told you to do only to wonder if it was him speaking in the first place. You've stared into a sky blackened with doubt. And you've asked what Joseph asked.

You've asked if you're still on the right road. You've asked if you were supposed to turn left when you turned right. And you've asked if there is a plan behind this scheme. Things haven't turned out like you thought they would.

Each of us knows what it's like to search the night for light. Not outside a stable, but perhaps outside an emergency room. On the gravel of a roadside. On the manicured grass of a cemetery. We've asked our questions. We questioned God's plan. And we've wondered why God does what he does.

The Bethlehem sky is not the first to hear the pleadings of a confused pilgrim.

If you are asking what Joseph asked, let me urge you to do what Joseph did. Obey. That's what he did. He obeyed. He obeyed when the angel called. He obeyed when Mary explained. He obeyed when God sent.

He was obedient to God.

He was obedient when the sky was bright.

He was obedient when the sky was dark.

He didn't let his confusion disrupt his obedience. He didn't know everything. But he did what he knew. He shut down his business, packed up his family, and went to another country. Why? Because that's what God said to do.

What about you? Just like Joseph, you can't see the whole picture. Just like Joseph your task is to see that Jesus is brought into your part of your world. And just like Joseph you have a choice: to obey or disobey. Because Joseph obeyed, God used him to change the world.

Can he do the same with you?

God still looks for Josephs today. Men and women who believe that God is not through with this world. Common people who serve an uncommon God.

Will you be that kind of person? Will you serve . . . even when you don't understand?

No, the Bethlehem sky is not the first to hear the pleadings of an honest heart, nor the last. And perhaps God didn't answer every question for Joseph. But he answered the most important one. "Are you still with me, God?" And through the first cries of the God-child the answer came.

"Yes. Yes, Joseph. I'm with you."

There are many questions about the Bible that we won't be

able to answer until we get home. Many knotholes and snapshots. Many times we will muse, "I wonder . . ."

But in our wonderings, there is one question we never need to ask. Does God care? Do we matter to God? Does he still love his children?

Through the small face of the stable-born baby, he says yes.

Yes, your sins are forgiven.

Yes, your name is written in heaven.

Yes, death has been defeated.

And yes, God has entered your world.

Immanuel. God is with us.

19

THE GRAVE FACT

Understanding Death

A man named Lazarus was sick. He lived in the town of Bethany, where Mary and her sister Martha lived. Mary was the woman who later put perfume on the Lord and wiped his feet with her hair. Mary's brother was Lazarus, the man who was now sick. So Mary and Martha sent someone to tell Jesus, "Lord, the one you love is sick."

When Jesus heard this, he said, "This sickness will not end in death. It is for the glory of God, to bring glory to the Son of God." Jesus loved Martha and her sister and Lazarus. But when he heard that Lazarus was sick, he stayed where he was for two more days. Then Jesus said to his followers, "Let's go back to Judea."

The followers said, "But Teacher, the Jews there tried to stone you to death only a short time ago. Now you want to go back there?"

Jesus answered, "Are there not twelve hours in the day? If anyone walks in the daylight, he will not stumble, because he can see by this world's light. But if anyone walks at night, he stumbles because there is no light to help him see."

After Jesus said this, he added, "Our friend Lazarus has fallen asleep, but I am going there to wake him."

The followers said, "But Lord, if he is only asleep, he will be all right."

Jesus meant that Lazarus was dead, but his followers thought he meant Lazarus was really sleeping. So then Jesus said plainly, "Lazarus is dead. And I am glad for your sakes I was not there so that you may believe. But let's go to him now."

Then Thomas (the one called Didymus) said to the other followers, "Let us also go so that we can die with him."

When Jesus arrived, he learned that Lazarus had already been dead and in the tomb for four days. Bethany was about two miles from Jerusalem. Many of the Jews had come there to comfort Martha and Mary about their brother.

When Martha heard that Jesus was coming, she went out to meet him, but Mary stayed home. Martha said to Jesus, "Lord, if you had been here, my brother would not have died. But I know that even now God will give you anything you ask."

Jesus said, "Your brother will rise and live again."

Martha answered, "I know that he will rise and live again in the resurrection on the last day."

Jesus said to her, "I am the resurrection and the life. Those who believe in me will have life even if they die. And everyone who lives and believes in me will never die. Martha, do you believe this?"

Martha answered, "Yes, Lord. I believe that you are the Christ, the Son of God, the One coming to the world."

After Martha said this, she went back and talked to her sister Mary alone. Martha said, "The Teacher is here and he is asking for you." When Mary heard this, she got up quickly and went to Jesus. Jesus had not yet come into the town but was still at the place where Martha had met him. The Jews were with Mary in the house, comforting her. When they saw her stand and leave quickly, they followed her, thinking she was going to the tomb to cry there. But Mary went to the place where Jesus was. When she saw him, she fell at his feet and said, "Lord, if you had been here, my brother would not have died."

When Jesus saw Mary crying and the Jews who came with her also crying, he was upset and was deeply troubled. He asked, "Where did you bury him?"

"Come and see, Lord," they said.

Jesus cried.

So the Jews said, "See how much he loved him."

But some of them said, "If Jesus opened the eyes of the blind man, why couldn't he keep Lazarus from dying?"

Again feeling very upset, Jesus came to the tomb. It was a cave with a large stone covering the entrance. Jesus said, "Move the stone away."

Martha, the sister of the dead man, said, "But, Lord, it has been four days since he died. There will be a bad smell."

Then Jesus said to her, "Didn't I tell you that if you believed you would see the glory of God?"

So they moved the stone away from the entrance. Then Jesus looked up and said, "Father, I thank you that you heard me. I know that you always hear me, but I said these things because of the people here around me. I want them to believe that you sent me." After Jesus said this, he cried out in a loud voice, "Lazarus, come out!" The dead man came out, his hands and feet wrapped with pieces of cloth, and a cloth around his face.

Jesus said to them, "Take the cloth off of him and let him go."

John 11:1–44

> Death, where is your victory?
>
> > 1 Corinthians 15:55

You are leaving the church building. The funeral is over. The burial is next. Ahead of you walk six men who carry the coffin that carries the body of your son. Your only son.

You're numb from the sorrow. Stunned. You lost your husband, and now you've lost your son. Now you have no family. If you had any more tears, you'd weep. If you had any more faith, you'd pray. But both are in short supply, so you do neither. You just stare at the back of the wooden box.

Suddenly it stops. The pallbearers have stopped. You stop.

A man has stepped in front of the casket. You don't know him. You've never seen him. He wasn't at the funeral. He's dressed in a corduroy coat and jeans. You have no idea what he is doing. But before you can object, he steps up to you and says, "Don't cry."

Don't cry? Don't cry! This is a funeral. My son is dead. Don't cry? Who are you to tell me not to cry? Those are your thoughts, but they never become your words. Because before you can speak, he acts.

He turns back to the coffin, places his hand on it, and says in a loud voice, "Young man, I tell you, get up!"

"Now just a minute," one of the pallbearers objects. But the sentence is interrupted by a sudden movement in the casket. The men look at one another and lower it quickly to the ground. It's

184

a good thing they do, because as soon as it touches the sidewalk the lid slowly opens . . .

Sound like something out of a science fiction novel? It's not. It's right out of the Gospel of Luke. "He went up and touched the coffin, and the people who were carrying it stopped. Jesus said, 'Young man, I tell you, get up!' And the son sat up and began to talk" (Luke 7:14–15).

Be careful now. Don't read that last line too fast. Try it again. Slowly.

"The son sat up and began to talk."

Incredible sentence, don't you think? At the risk of overdoing it, let's read it one more time. This time say each word aloud. "The son sat up and began to talk."

Good job. (Did everyone around you look up?) Can we do it again? This time read it aloud again, but very s-l-o-w-l-y. Pause between each word.

"The . . . son . . . sat . . . up . . . and . . . began . . . to . . . talk."

Now the question. What's odd about that verse?

You got it. Dead people don't sit up! Dead people don't talk! Dead people don't leave their coffins!

Unless Jesus shows up. Because when Jesus shows up, you never know what might happen.

Jairus can tell you. His daughter was already dead. The mourners were already in the house. The funeral had begun. The people thought the best Jesus could do was offer some kind words about Jairus's girl. Jesus had some words all right. Not about the girl, but for the girl.

"My child, stand up!" (Luke 8:54).

The next thing the father knew, she was eating, Jesus was laughing, and the hired mourners were sent home early.

Martha can tell you. She'd hoped Jesus would show up to heal Lazarus. He didn't. Then she'd hoped he'd show up to bury Lazarus. He didn't. By the time he made it to Bethany, Lazarus was four-days buried and Martha was wondering what kind of friend Jesus was.

She hears he's at the edge of town so she storms out to meet him. "Lord, if you had been here," she confronts, "my brother would not have died" (John 11:21).

There is hurt in those words. Hurt and disappointment. The one man who could have made a difference didn't, and Martha wants to know why.

Maybe you do, too. Maybe you've done what Martha did. Someone you love ventures near the edge of life, and you turn to Jesus for help. You, like Martha, turn to the only one who can pull a person from the ledge of death. You ask Jesus to give a hand.

Martha must have thought, *Surely he will come. Didn't he aid the paralytic? Didn't he help the leper? Didn't he give sight to the blind? And they hardly knew Jesus. Lazarus is his friend. We're like family. Doesn't Jesus come for the weekend? Doesn't he eat at our table? When he hears that Lazarus is sick, he'll be here in a heartbeat.*

But he didn't come. Lazarus got worse. She watched out the window. Jesus didn't show. Her brother drifted in and out of consciousness. "He'll be here soon, Lazarus," she promised. "Hang on."

But the knock at the door never came. Jesus never appeared. Not to help. Not to heal. Not to bury. And now, four days later, he finally shows up. The funeral is over. The body is buried, and the grave is sealed.

And Martha is hurt.

Her words have been echoed in a thousand cemeteries. "If you had been here, my brother would not have died."

If you were doing your part, God, my husband would have survived. If you'd done what was right, Lord, my baby would have lived.

If only you'd have heard my prayer, God, my arms wouldn't be empty.

The grave unearths our view of God.

When we face death, our definition of God is challenged. Which, in turn, challenges our faith. Which leads me to ask a grave question. Why is it that we interpret the presence of death as the absence of God? Why do we think that if the body is not healed then God is not near? Is healing the only way God demonstrates his presence?

Sometimes we think so. And as a result, when God doesn't answer our prayers for healing, we get angry. Resentful. Blame replaces belief. "If you had been here, doing your part, God, then this death would not have happened."

It's distressing that this view of God has no place for death.

Some time ago a visitor to our house showed my daughters some tricks. Magic acts. Simple sleight-of-hand stuff. I stood to the side and watched the girls' responses. They were amazed. When the coin disappeared, they gasped. When it reappeared, they were stunned. At first I was humored by their bewilderment.

But with time, my bewilderment became concern. Part of me didn't like what was happening. My kids were being duped. He was tricking them. They, the innocent, were being buffaloed by him, the sneak. I didn't like that. I didn't like seeing my children fooled.

So I whispered to my daughters. "It's in his sleeve." Sure enough it was. "It's behind his ear." And what do you know, I was right! Maybe I was rude to interfere with the show, but I don't enjoy watching a trickster pull one over on my children.

Neither does God.

Jesus couldn't bear to sit and watch the bereaved be fooled.

Please understand, he didn't raise the dead for the sake of the dead. He raised the dead for the sake of the living.

"Lazarus, come out!" (v. 43).

Martha was silent as Jesus commanded. The mourners were quiet. No one stirred as Jesus stood face to face with the rock-hewn tomb and demanded that it release his friend.

No one stirred, that is, except for Lazarus. Deep within the tomb, he moved. His stilled heart began to beat again. Wrapped eyes popped open. Wooden fingers lifted. And a mummied man in a tomb sat up. And want to know what happened next?

Let John tell you. "The dead man came out, his hands and feet wrapped with pieces of cloth, and a cloth around his face" (v. 44).

There it is again. Did you see it? Read the first five words of the verse again.

"The dead man came out."

Again. Slower this time.

"The dead man came out."

One more time. This time out loud and very slowly. (I know you think I'm crazy, but I really want you to get the point.)

"The . . . dead . . . man . . . came . . . out."

Can I ask the same questions? (Of course I can; I'm writing the book!)

Question: What's wrong with this picture?

Answer: Dead men don't walk out of tombs.

Question: What kind of God is this?

Answer: The God who holds the keys to life and death.

The kind of God who rolls back the sleeve of the trickster and reveals death for the parlor trick it is.

The kind of God you want present at your funeral.

He'll do it again, you know. He's promised he would. And he's shown that he can.

"The Lord himself will come down from heaven with a loud command" (1 Thess. 4:16).

The same voice that awoke the boy near Nain, that stirred the still daughter of Jairus, that awakened the corpse of Lazarus—the same voice will speak again. The earth and the sea will give up their dead. There will be no more death.

Jesus made sure of that.

20

LISTLESS CHRISTIANITY

When Being Good Is Not Enough

When they came to a place called the Skull, the soldiers cruci-
fied Jesus and the criminals—one on his right and the other on
his left. Jesus said, "Father, forgive them, because they don't
know what they are doing."

The soldiers threw lots to decide who would get his clothes.
The people stood there watching. And the leaders made fun of
Jesus, saying, "He saved others. Let him save himself if he is
God's Chosen One, the Christ."

The soldiers also made fun of him, coming to Jesus and
offering him some vinegar. They said, "If you are the king of the
Jews, save yourself!" At the top of the cross these words were
written: THIS IS THE KING OF THE JEWS.

One of the criminals on a cross began to shout insults at
Jesus: "Aren't you the Christ? Then save yourself and us."

But the other criminal stopped him and said, "You should
fear God! You are getting the same punishment he is. We are
punished justly, getting what we deserve for what we did. But
this man has done nothing wrong." Then he said, "Jesus,
remember me when you come into your kingdom."

Luke 23:33–42

> "I tell you the truth, today you will be
> with me in paradise."
>
> Luke 23:43

She nearly missed the flight. In fact, I thought I had the row to myself when I looked up and saw her puffing down the aisle, dragging two large bags.

"I hate to fly," she blurted out as she fell into her seat. "I put off getting here as long as I can."

"You almost put it off too long," I smiled.

She was tall, young, blonde, tan, and talkative. Her jeans were fashionably ripped at the knees. And her black boots boasted silver tips. She really did hate to fly, I learned. And the way she coped with flying was by talking.

"I'm going home to see my dad. He'll really be amazed at my tan. He thinks I'm crazy living in California—me being single and all. I've got this new boyfriend, he's from Lebanon. He travels a lot though, so I only see him on weekends, which is fine with me because that gives me the house to myself. It isn't far from the beach and . . ."

I've learned what to do when a friendly, attractive woman sits beside me. As soon as possible I reveal my profession and marital status. It keeps us both out of trouble.

"My *wife* hates to fly, too," I jumped in when she took a breath, "so I know how you feel. And since I'm a *minister,* I know a section of the Bible you might like to read as we take off."

191

I pulled out my Bible from my briefcase and opened it to Psalm 23.

For the first time she was quiet. "The Lord is my shepherd," she read the words then looked up with a broad smile. "I remember this," she said as the plane was taking off. "I read it when I was young."

She turned to read some more. The next time she looked up there was a tear in her eye.

"It's been a long time. A long, long time." She told me how she believed . . . once. She became a Christian when she was young, but she couldn't remember the last time she'd been to church.

We talked some about faith and second chances. I asked her if I could ask her a question. She said I could.

"Do you believe in heaven?"

"Yeah."

"Do you think you'll go there?"

She looked away for a minute and then turned and answered confidently, "Yeah. Yeah, I'll be in heaven."

"How do you know?"

"How do I know I'm going to heaven?" She grew quiet as she formulated her response.

Somehow I knew what she was going to say before she said it. I could see it coming. She was going to give me her "list." (Everybody has one.)

"Well, I'm basically good. I don't smoke more than a pack a day. I exercise. I'm dependable at work and," she counted each achievement on a finger, "I made my boyfriend get tested for AIDS."

Ta-da. That was her list. Her qualifications. By her way of thinking, heaven could be earned by good health habits and safe sex. Her line of logic was simple—I keep the list on earth and I get the place in heaven.

Now lest we be too hard on her, let me ask you a question. What's on your list?

Most of us have one. Most of us are like the girl on the plane. We think we are "basically good." Decent, hardworking folk. Most of us have a list to prove it. Maybe yours doesn't include cigarettes or AIDS. But you have a list.

"I pay my bills."

"I love my spouse and kids."

"I attend church."

"I'm better than Hitler."

"I'm basically good."

Most of us have a list. There is a purpose for the list: to prove we are good. But there is a problem with the list: none of us is good enough.

Paul made this point when he placed two short-fused sticks of dynamite in the third chapter of his letter to the Romans. The first is in verse 10. "There is no one who always does what is right," he wrote, "not even one." No one. Not you. Not me. Not anyone. The second explosion occurs in verse 23. "All have sinned and are not good enough for God's glory."

Boom. So much for lists. So much for being "basically good."

Then how do you go to heaven? If no one is good, if no list is sufficient, if no achievements are adequate, how can a person be saved?

No question is more crucial. To hear Jesus answer it, let's ponder the last encounter he had before his death. An encounter between Jesus and two criminals.

All three are being crucified.

One might like to think that these two thieves are victims. Undeserving of punishment. Good men who got a bad rap. Patriots dying a martyr's death. But such is not the case. Matthew dispels any such notion with just one verse, "the robbers who were being crucified beside Jesus also insulted him" (Matt. 27:44).

Tragedy reveals a person's character. And the tragedy of this crucifixion reveals that these two thieves had none. They slander Jesus with their last breaths. Can you hear them? Voices—husky with pain—sneer at the Messiah.

"Some king of the Jews you are."

"Life is pretty tough on Messiahs these days, eh?"

"How about a little miracle, Galilean?"

"Ever see nails that size in Nazareth?"

You'd expect it from the Pharisees. You'd expect it from the crowd. Even the mocking of the soldiers isn't surprising. But from the thieves?

Crucified men insulting a crucified man? It's two men with nooses on their necks ridiculing the plight of a third. Two POWs before a firing squad taunting another's misfortune.

Could anyone be more blind?

Could anyone be more vile?

No wonder these two are on the cross! Rome deems them worthy of ugly torture. Their only value to society is to serve as a public spectacle. Strip them naked so all will know that evil cannot hide. Nail their hands so all will see that the wicked have no strength. Post them high so all will tell their children, "That's what happens to evil men."

Every muscle in their bodies screams for relief. Nails pulse fire through their arms. Legs contort and twist seeking comfort.

But there is no comfort on a cross.

Yet even the pain of the spike won't silence their spiteful tongues. These two will die as they lived, attacking the innocent. But in this case, the innocent doesn't retaliate.

The man they mocked wasn't much to look at. His body was whip-torn flesh, yanked away from the bone. His face was a mask of blood and spit; eyes puffy and swollen. "King of the Jews" was painted over his head. A crown of thorns pierced his scalp. His lip was split. Maybe his nose was bleeding or a tooth was loose.

The man they mocked was half-dead. The man they mocked was beaten. But the man they mocked was at peace. "Father, forgive them, because they don't know what they are doing" (Luke 23:34).

After Jesus' prayer, one of the criminals began to shout insults at him: "Aren't you the Christ? Then save yourself and us" (v. 39).

The heart of this thief remains hard. The presence of Christ crucified means nothing to him. Jesus is worthy of ridicule, so the thief ridicules. He expects his chorus to be harmonized from the other cross. It isn't. Instead, it is challenged.

"You should fear God! You are getting the same punishment he is. We are punished justly, getting what we deserve for what we did. But this man has done nothing wrong" (vv. 40–41).

Unbelievable. The same mouth that cursed Christ now defends Christ. What has happened? What has he seen since he has been on the cross? Did he witness a miracle? Did he hear a lecture? Was he read a treatise on the trinity?

No, of course not. According to Luke, all he heard was a prayer, a prayer of grace. But that was enough. Something happens to a man who stands in the presence of God. And something happened to the thief.

Read again his words. "We are punished justly, getting what we deserve. . . . But this man has done nothing wrong."

The core of the gospel in one sentence. The essence of eternity through the mouth of a crook:

I am wrong; Jesus is right.

I have failed; Jesus has not.

I deserve to die; Jesus deserves to live.

The thief knew precious little about Christ, but what he knew was precious indeed. He knew that an innocent man was dying an unjust death with no complaint on his lips. And if Jesus can do that, he just might be who he says he is.

So the thief asks for help: "Jesus, remember me when you come into your kingdom."

The heavy head of Christ lifts and turns, and the eyes of these two meet. What Jesus sees is a naked man. I don't mean in terms of clothes. I mean in terms of charades. He has no cover. No way to hide.

His title? Scum of the earth. His achievement? Death by crucifixion. His reputation? Criminal. His character? Depraved until the last moment. Until the final hour. Until the last encounter.

Until now.

195

Tell me, what has this man done to warrant help? He has wasted his life. Who is he to beg for forgiveness? He publicly scoffed at Jesus. What right does he have to pray this prayer?

Do you really want to know? The same right you have to pray yours.

You see, that is you and me on the cross. Naked, desolate, hopeless, and estranged. That is us. That is us asking, "In spite of what I've done, in spite of what you see, is there any way you could remember me when we all get home?"

We don't boast. We don't produce our list. Any sacrifice appears silly when placed before God on a cross.

It's more than we deserve. But we are desperate. So we plead. As have so many others: The cripple at the pool. Mary at the wedding. Martha at the funeral. The demoniac at Geresene. Nicodemus at night. Peter on the sea. Jairus on the trail. Joseph at the stable. And every other human being who has dared to stand before the Son of God and admit his or her need.

We, like the thief, have one more prayer. And we, like the thief, pray.

And we, like the thief, hear the voice of grace. *Today you will be with me in my kingdom.*

And we, like the thief, are able to endure the pain knowing he'll soon take us home.

21

THE STONE MOVER'S GALLERY

Quite a gallery, don't you think? A room of pain-to-peace portraits. A ward of renewed strength. A forest of restored vigor.

An exhibition of second chances.

Wouldn't it be incredible to visit a real one? Wouldn't it be great to walk through an actual collection of "Bruised Reeds and Smoldering Wicks"? What if you could see portrayal after portrayal of God meeting people at their points of pain? Not just biblical characters, but contemporary folks just like you? People from your generation and your world!

And what if this gallery contained not only their story, but yours and mine as well? What if there were a place where you could display our "before" and "after" experiences? Well, there might be one. I have an idea for such a gallery. It may sound far-fetched, but it's worth sharing.

Before I do, we need to discuss one final question. A crucial question. You've just read one story after another of God meeting people where they hurt. Tell me, why are these stories in the Bible? Why are the Gospels full of such people? Such hopeless people? Though their situations vary, their conditions don't. They are trapped. Estranged. Rejected. They have nowhere to turn. On their lips, a desperate prayer. In their hearts, desolate dreams. And in their hands, a broken rope. But before their eyes a never-say-die Galilean who majors in stepping in when everyone else steps out.

Surprisingly simple, the actions of this man. Just words of mercy or touches of kindness. Fingers on sightless eyes. A hand on a weary shoulder. Words for sad hearts . . . all fulfilling the prophecy: "A bruised reed he will not break, and a smoldering wick he will not snuff out."

Again I ask. Why are these portraits in the Bible? Why does this gallery exist? Why did God leave us one tale after another of wounded lives being restored? So we could be grateful for the past? So we could look back with amazement at what Jesus did?

No. No. No. A thousand times no. The purpose of these stories is not to tell us what Jesus *did*. Their purpose is to tell us what Jesus *does*.

"Everything that was written in the past was written to teach us," Paul penned. "The Scriptures give us patience and encouragement so that we can have hope" (Rom. 15:4).

These are not just Sunday school stories. Not romantic fables. Not somewhere-over-the-rainbow illusions. They are historic moments in which a real God met real pain so we could answer the question, "Where is God when I hurt?"

How does God react to dashed hopes? Read the story of Jairus. How does the Father feel about those who are ill? Stand with him at the pool of Bethesda. Do you long for God to speak to your lonely heart? Then listen as he speaks to the Emmaus-bound disciples. What is God's word for the shameful? Watch as his finger draws in the dirt of the Jerusalem courtyard.

He's not doing it just for them. He's doing it for me. He's doing it for you.

Which takes us to the final painting in the gallery—yours. Now that you've finished the book, pick up the brush. Now that you've read their stories, reflect on yours. Stand in front of the canvases that bear your name and draw your portraits.

It doesn't have to be on a canvas with paint. It could be on a paper with pencil, on a computer with words, in a sculpture with clay, in a song with lyrics. It doesn't matter how you do it, but I urge you to do it. Record your drama. Retell your saga. Plot your journey.

Begin with "before." What was it like before you knew him? Do you remember? Could be decades ago. Perhaps it was yesterday. Maybe you know him well. Maybe you've just met him. Again, that doesn't matter. What matters is that you never forget what life is like without him.

Remembering can hurt. Parts of our past are not pleasant to revisit. But the recollection is necessary. "Look at what you were when God called you," Paul instructed (1 Cor. 1:26). We, the adopted, can't forget what life was like as orphans. We, the liberated, should revisit the prison. We, the found, can't forget the despair of being lost.

Amnesia fosters arrogance. We can't afford to forget. We need to remember.

And we need to share our story. Not with everyone but with someone. There is someone who is like you were. And he or she needs to know what God can do. Your honest portrayal of your past may be the courage for another's future.

But don't just portray the past, depict the present. Describe his touch. Display the difference he has made in your life. This task has its challenges, too. Whereas painting the "before" can be painful, painting the "present" can be unclear. He's not finished with you yet!

Ah, but look how far you've come! I don't even know you, but I know you've come a long way. Wasn't there a time when you wouldn't even pick up a Christian book? And now look at you; you've almost finished one! God has begun a work in your heart. And what God begins, God completes. "God began doing a good work in you, and I am sure he will continue it until it is finished when Jesus Christ comes again" (Phil. 1:6).

So chronicle what Christ has done. If he has brought peace, sketch a dove. If joy, splash a rainbow on a wall. If courage, sing a song about mountain-movers. And when you're finished, don't hide it away. Put it where you can see it. Put it where you can be reminded, daily, of the Father's tender power.

And when we all get home, we'll make a gallery.

That's my idea. I know it's crazy, but what if, when we all get home, we make a gallery? I don't know if they allow this kind of stuff in heaven. But something tells me the Father won't mind. After all, there's plenty of space and lots of time.

And what an icebreaker! What a way to make friends! Can you envision it? There's Jonah with a life-size whale. Moses in front of a blazing bush. David is giving slingshot lessons. Gideon is letting people touch the fleece—*the* fleece—and Abraham is describing a painting entitled, "The Night with a Thousand Stars."

You can sit with Zacchaeus in his tree. A young boy shows you a basket of five loaves and two fishes. Martha welcomes you in her kitchen. The Centurion invites you to touch the cross.

Martin Luther is there with the Book of Romans. Susannah Wesley tells how she prayed for her sons—Charles and John. Dwight Moody tells of the day he left the shoe store to preach. And John Newton volunteers to sing "Amazing Grace" with an angelic backup.

Some are famous, most are not . . . but all are heroes. A soldier lets you sit in a foxhole modeled after the one he was in when he met Christ. A housewife shows you her tear-stained New Testament. Beside a Nigerian is the missionary who taught him. And behind the Brazilian is a drawing of the river in which he was baptized.

And somewhere in the midst of this arena of hope is your story. Person after person comes. They listen as if they have all the time in the world. (And they do!) They treat you as if you are royalty. (For you are!) Solomon asks you questions. Job compliments your stamina. Joshua lauds your courage. And when they all applaud, you applaud too. For in heaven, everyone knows that all praise goes to one source.

And speaking of the source, he's represented in the heavenly gallery as well. Turn and look. High above the others. In the most prominent place. Exactly in the middle. There is one display elevated high on a platform above the others. Visible from any point in the gallery is a boulder. It's round. It's heavy. It used to seal the opening of a tomb.

But not anymore. Ask Mary and Mary. Ask Peter. Ask Lazarus. Ask anyone in the gallery. They'll tell you. Stones were never a match for God.

Will there be such a gallery in heaven? Who knows? But I do know there used to be a stone in front of a tomb. And I do know it was moved. And I also know that there are stones in your path. Stones that trip and stones that trap. Stones too big for you.

Please remember, the goal of these stories is not to help us look back with amazement, but forward with faith. The God who spoke still speaks. The God who forgave still forgives. The God who came still comes. He comes into our world. He comes into your world. He comes to do what you can't. He comes to move the stones you can't budge.

Stones are no match for God. Not then and not now. He still moves stones.

Study Guide

Chapter 1 • Bruised Reeds and Smoldering Wicks

Looking Under the Stones:

1. Describe the appearance of a bruised reed and a smoldering wick. What makes them both so fragile, so close to death? In what way can people be like bruised reeds or smoldering wicks?

2. Describe a time you have felt like a bruised reed or a smoldering wick. What were the circumstances? How did things turn out?

3. Discuss Max's comments: "The world has a place for the beaten. The world will break you off; the world will snuff you out. But the artists of Scripture proclaim that God won't." Do you find his observations to be true? Explain your answer.

4. Max claims that God is "the friend of the wounded heart . . . the keeper of your dreams" and that he "has a special place for the bruised and weary of the world." What do you think he means by this? Describe a time in your life when you experienced the truth of his words.

5. Are there any "bruised reeds" or "smoldering wicks" in your life right now? If so, how do you handle them? What do you say? Do? How can the message of *He Still Moves Stones* instruct you on how to treat such fragile people?

6. Finish the following sentence: "The fact that Jesus doesn't break bruised reeds and doesn't snuff out smoldering wicks makes me _____."

Building on the Rock:

1. Read Matthew 12:15–21.

   a. How does verse 15 fulfill Isaiah's prophecy quoted in verse 20?

   b. How does verse 16 fulfill Isaiah's prophecy quoted in verse 19?

   c. In what way did Jesus fulfill Isaiah's prophecy quoted in verse 21? What does it mean to "find hope" in Jesus? Have you done this?

2. Read Luke 4:14–21.

   a. How is the prophecy quoted in verses 18–19 like the prophecy quoted in Matthew 12? How is it different?

   b. What did Jesus mean in verse 21? How had this prophecy been "fulfilled"? If it really had been fulfilled, what would this mean about the identity of Jesus?

Chapter 2 • Not Guilty

Looking Under the Stones:

1. In what way did Rebecca Thompson "die" twice? Do you know of anyone who has "died" as Rebecca did the first time? If so, describe the situation.

2. No one can know for sure why Rebecca jumped. What do you think drove her to suicide? Fear? Anger? Guilt? Shame? Explain your answer.

3. Max writes, "Whether private or public, shame is always painful. And unless you deal with it, it is permanent. Unless you get help—the dawn will never come." What do you think he

means? Do you agree with him? Why or why not?

4. What does the word *shame* mean to you? What does the word *grace* mean to you? Which is the stronger term? Why?

5. With what character in the story of John 8 do you identify most closely? The woman? The guilty (but absent) man? The Pharisees? The men in the crowd? Jesus? Explain your choice.

6. The Scripture doesn't say, but what do you think Jesus may have been writing in the sand?

7. Jesus told the woman, "I also don't judge you guilty. You may go now, but don't sin anymore" (John 8:11). Does any part of this statement bother you? Is it what you would have expected Jesus to say? Why?

8. Do the words "not guilty" apply to you? Explain your answer. How do those words make you feel?

Building on the Rock:

1. Read John 8:1–11.

   a. What was the trap the Pharisees were trying to lay for Jesus? What did they want him to do? How did he avoid their trap?

   b. Verse 9 says "those who heard [Jesus' answer] began to go away one at a time, the older ones first." Why do you think the older ones left first? Why is this an important detail?

2. Read Romans 8:1–9.

   a. In what way does this text explain the phrase "not guilty"? According to Romans 8, to whom does it apply?

b. How does verse 9 explain how the woman caught in adultery could comply with Jesus' command to her in John 8:11?

Chapter 3 • Don't Miss the Party

Looking Under the Stones:

1. What was the elder son's basic problem? Have you ever felt the way he did? If so, what were the circumstances?

2. Give your own definition of *bitterness*.

3. Do you know anyone whose life is marked by bitterness? If so, what is it like to be around that person? What lessons have you learned from him or her?

4. What does Max mean when he writes, "what you have is more important than what you don't have"? Is he right? Why or why not?

5. Did it surprise you to learn that Stephen A. Douglas was Abraham Lincoln's closest friend? If so, why? In what way is Lincoln a good example of the central truth of this chapter? In what way is he a good model for us?

6. Max writes that "no pouters are permitted" at God's final celebration. If God were to call us to his party today, would you be ready? Explain your answer.

7. Why don't some people "come and join the fun"? What reasons do they give? Did you ever give such reasons? If so, what were they? What convinced you to change your mind?

Building on the Rock:

1. Read Luke 15:11–32.

a. With whom do you most identify in this story? The younger son? The older son? The father? The servants? The fat calf? Explain your answer.

b. How did the father react to the younger son's speech in verse 21? How is this significant? What might it suggest to you about your own prayer life?

c. How does verse 32 help to color our understanding of Luke 15:10?

2. Read Hebrews 12:14–15.

a. What connection is there in verse 14 between living in peace with all people and being holy? Which one logically comes first?

b. What is the connection in verse 15 between "God's grace" and a "bitter root"? What does the grace of God do? What does a bitter root do?

c. In what ways do the story of Luke 15:11–32 illustrate the truths of Hebrews 12:14–15?

Chapter 4 • *When You and Your Kin Can't*

Looking Under the Stones:

1. Give a word picture to describe a relative in *your* life who really bugs you.

2. Do you have any "tar-baby relatives"? If so, what makes it hard to communicate with them?

3. Why *does* life get so "relatively difficult"? What can you do when those closest to you keep their distance?

4. How does it make you feel that Jesus himself had a difficult family? What was your reaction when you first read such a statement?

5. What do you think Jesus meant when he said, "A prophet is honored everywhere except in his hometown and in his own home" (Matt. 13:57)?

6. Go back through the chapter and list the many ways Jesus' family dishonored him. How did Jesus react to these insults? What can we learn from these incidents?

7. Max writes, "It's worth noting that [Jesus] didn't try to control his family's behavior, nor did he let their behavior control his." In what way is this an excellent principle for us?

8. How did the members of Jesus' family finally change in their appraisal of him? How can this give us hope?

Building on the Rock:

1. Read Psalm 139:5, Matthew 6:25–34, Galatians 4:7, Ephesians 1:5, and 1 John 3:1.

   a. What do these verses tell us about God as our Father? What does each one mean to you?

   b. If you have other favorite verses that describe God as your Father, list them. Why are these personal favorites?

2. Compare Romans 14:14–15:4 with 1 Corinthians 10:29–30.

   a. What light do these passages shed on our ability to withstand both our family's attempts to control us as well as our desire to control the behavior of our family?

b. In what way is Romans 14:19 generally a good prescription for harmony in the family? How about Romans 15:2? In what instances must other principles also be considered?

Chapter 5 • *It's All Right to Dream Again*

Looking Under the Stones:

1. Max writes, "there are times when we, too, are called to love, expecting nothing in return." What sort of times like this can you recall?

2. Discuss the following statement: "Service prompted by duty. This is the call of discipleship."

3. Does the fact that the angel rolled the stone away from the Lord's tomb imply anything significant for your own life? If so, what?

4. Describe some times in your life when God has proven to be a God of surprises.

5. What challenges face you right now in which the words "don't give up" are especially appropriate?

6. How does it make you feel that God is watching you and your circumstances?

7. In what ways does the resurrection breathe new life into your own hopes and dreams?

Building on the Rock:

1. Read Matthew 28:1–15.

   a. Why do you think the angel not only rolled away the stone but then sat on it (v. 2)? Why do you think he spoke to the women and not to the guards?

b. Why would the women be "afraid but they were also very happy" as verse 8 tells us?

c. What logical flaws can you spot in the fabricated story described in verse 13?

2. Read Galatians 6:9.

a. What command is given in this verse? Why does it seem so easy for us to ignore this command? What promise is given to us when we comply with the command?

b. How are the two Marys good illustrations of the truth of this verse?

3. Read Hebrews 10:32–38.

a. What is the purpose of the "history lesson" in verses 32–34? If the writer were describing your own experience rather than that of the Hebrews, what would he have written?

b. What command is given in verse 35? What related promise is described? How is this promise further explained in verse 36?

c. How is the prophecy of verse 37 intended to help us persevere? In what way does this prophecy encourage you?

Chapter 6 • Sour Milk

Looking Under the Stones:

1. Max writes, "Sweet milk turns sour from being too warm, too long. Sweet dispositions turn sour for the same reason." Explain what this means to you.

2. Are you more likely to follow Mary or Martha's example? Are you satisfied with this? Why? If you think you need to change, describe what you can do to bring about that change.

3. Do you know of a situation where someone's work for the Lord became more important than the Lord himself? Has this ever happened to you? If so, describe what happened.

4. Discuss the following statement: "God is more pleased with the quiet attention of a sincere servant than the noisy service of a sour one."

5. Why is it so easy for most of us to forget who is the servant and who is to be served?

6. What steps do you take to ensure that your focus doesn't become stuck on yourself?

7. When was the last time you took a break simply to "sit at the feet of Jesus"? Describe what you did and how it affected your behavior and attitudes afterward.

8. Discuss the joke about the fellow who prayed with a bad attitude on page 62. Have you ever prayed this prayer? What did you think of God's answer to the man's prayer?

Building on the Rock:

1. Read Luke 10:38–42.

   a. What was the Lord talking about when he told Martha that "only one thing is important" in verse 42? What is this "one thing"? Does it exist in your life?

   b. What is significant about the Lord's words, "Mary has *chosen* the better thing"? How does this comment relate to your own Christian walk?

   c. What promise is made in verse 42? How does this promise also apply to us?

2. Read Matthew 21:28–32.

   a. What does this parable teach us about service? What lesson might Martha have learned from it?

   b. Which of the two sons do you resemble?

   c. What point is Jesus making in verses 31–32? Why does he sound so harsh here?

Chapter 7 • A Crazy Hunch and a High Hope

Looking Under the Stones:

1. What was the crazy hunch and the high hope of the woman in Mark 5? In specific terms, how can she be an example for us today?

2. Discuss Max's definition of faith: "A conviction that [God] can and a hope that he will."

3. Max writes, "Faith is not the belief that God will do what you want. Faith is the belief that God will do what is right." How should this change the way you pray? Does it?

4. Do you believe that "the more hopeless your circumstance, the more likely your salvation"? Why or why not?

5. Is it true that "faith with no effort is no faith at all"? Explain your answer.

6. Look over Max's "to do" list on page 69. Is there anything on the list that you need to do? Is there something that true faith would require you to do that isn't on that list? If so, what?

7. What is significant about the fact that Jesus called the afflicted woman "daughter"? Does this mean anything for your own relationship with Jesus?

Building on the Rock:

1. Read Mark 5:24–34.

   a. Why was it important for Jesus to find out who had touched his clothes? Why not just continue on his way?

   b. Why did the woman fall at Jesus' feet and tremble with fear? Is this the reaction you would expect? Why or why not?

2. Read Hebrews 11:1–6.

   a. How does the writer of Hebrews define faith? How would you describe it in your own terms?

   b. How are Abel and Enoch good examples of people of faith? How did they demonstrate their faith?

   c. How does the certainty of "reward" increase our faith (v. 6)?

3. Read James 2:14–26.

   a. Is it accurate to say that the writer of Hebrews *defines* faith and that James *illustrates* it? Explain your answer.

   b. Discuss the following: "Faith is not deeds, but faith produces deeds." Would James agree with this statement? Why or why not?

Chapter 8 • Forever Young

Looking Under the Stones:

1. When was the first time you specifically recall "the dawning of old age" in your own life? What happened? How does getting older make you feel?

2. Why does growing older sometimes spawn regrets? Try to name some examples of this.

3. How do regrets sometimes lead to rebellion? How can this process be short-circuited?

4. Max writes that there are two options as we grow older: safety vs. adventure. What does he mean and how do these two options play out in real life?

5. How can we "reclaim curiosity"? What advantages are there in doing so?

6. Max writes that Abraham, Moses, Caleb, Anna, and John all had one important thing in common. What was it? How can this be an encouragement to us?

7. When asked why he had taken up the study of Greek at the age of ninety-four, Oliver Wendell Holmes is reputed to have said, "Well, my good sir, it's now or never." What attitude do you suppose prompted Holmes to make such a statement? Do you admire him for it? Explain your answer.

8. Max writes, "As we get older, our vision should improve." What does this mean? Do you think it's true of your own experience? Why or why not?

Building on the Rock:

1. Read Luke 17:20–37.

    a. Jesus' saying, "Whoever tries to keep his life will lose it, and whoever loses his life will preserve it" is found in the middle of a discussion on planetary conditions as history draws to a close. Why is this significant? In what way does this seem especially significant for those who are growing older?

    b. How is Lot's wife a chilling example of Luke 17:33? (See Gen. 19:12–26.)

2. Read Titus 2:2–5.

    a. According to verse 2, what are the special duties of older men?

    b. According to verses 3–5, what are the special duties of older women?

Chapter 9 • Read the Story

Looking Under the Stones:

1. How does P. T. Barnum's saying, "There's a sucker born every minute," remind you of a hurt, heartbroken little boy?

2. Try to recall the first time you were heartbroken. How did you respond? How long did it take you to recover? What did friends or family do to help you recover?

3. Max writes, "Disappointment . . . will blind you to the very presence of God." How did this happen with the two men on the road to Emmaus? How does this happen with you?

4. In what ways does despair harden our hearts and make us cynical and calloused? Why is this dangerous?

5. Max writes that those with broken hearts are tempted to stop loving, stop trusting, and stop giving their hearts away. Have you ever seen people react in this way? If so, what did they do? Why do you suppose they did it?

6. Jesus did two things for the men on the road to Emmaus: (1) He came to them where they were; and (2) He told them the story of God. How is this formula still the cure for broken hearts? Does this mean the cure is easy? Explain.

7. Unfulfilled expectations are at the root of most heartbreaks. Why?

8. How can the knowledge that God is still in control affect our outlook when our heart is broken?

Building on the Rock:

1. Read Luke 24:13–35.

   a. ". . . but we were hoping," said Cleopas in verse 21. How does this phrase sum up his deep heartbreak?

   b. The most amazing Bible lesson in history is described in verse 27. What specific passages do you suppose Jesus quoted in this lesson?

2. Read Psalm 135:5–14 and Daniel 4:34–35.

   a. What picture of God do you get in Psalm 135?

   b. What picture of God do you get in Daniel 4?

   c. How do these pictures help us in times of heartbreak?

Chapter 10 • The Power of a Timid Prayer

Looking Under the Stones:

1. Are your prayers more of the Concorde or of the crop-duster variety? Explain.

2. Max writes that prayer begins as a yearning. A yearning for what? Is this true for you? If so, in what way?

3. What reasons do we give for not praying as we think we should? What reasons seem to be your "favorites"?

4. The man in Mark 9:24 prayed, "I do believe! Help me to believe more." Is this a prayer of faith? Is it an admirable prayer? Do you ever pray like this? Explain.

5. In what way did Jim Redmond's act at the 1992 Barcelona Olympics illustrate what our heavenly Father does for us? Describe the last time you received the Father's help in this way.

6. Discuss Max's statement that "the power of prayer is in the one who hears it and not the one who says it." What does this imply for our prayer life? Does it imply that our character makes no difference to God when it comes to answering our prayers? Explain.

7. Whether you're a crop duster or a Concorde, do you want to improve your prayer life? What specific steps can you take to do so?

Building on the Rock:

1. Read Mark 9:14–29.

    a. In what way was the man's comment, "*If* you can do anything" conditioned by his experience with Jesus' disciples? How do our actions affect unbelievers' opinions of Jesus?

b. How are Jesus' words in verse 25 specifically crafted to show his power and authority? How is this healing of a demoniac different from others recorded in Scripture?

2. Read Nehemiah 2:1–9.

a. Does the prayer alluded to in verse 4 belong to the Concorde or crop-duster variety? Was it answered? How is this significant?

b. What connection is there between the prayer of 2:4 and Nehemiah's actions in chapter 1? What should this teach us about our own prayer life?

Chapter 11 • Bright Lights on Dark Nights

Looking Under the Stones:

1. How often do you deliberately choose to be among the suffering? Is Jesus' presence at the pool of Bethesda an encouragement to you or a rebuke—or both? Explain.

2. In what way is the sick man's story really a tale about you and me?

3. Max writes, "we must admit we are like the paralytic. Invalids out of options." What does he mean by this? Do you agree with him? Why or why not?

4. Comment on this statement: "In God's plan, God is the standard for perfection . . . The goal is to be like him; anything less is inadequate." Identify some Scripture passages that say this in another way.

5. Why does it seem easier for an army private to believe the word of Alexander the Great (see page 111) than it does for us to believe the word of Jesus Christ?

6. Is Jesus telling you today, like the paralytic, to "stand up" in any area of your life? If so, what? If he is, what do you plan to do about it?

Building on the Rock:

1. Read Romans 3:9–23.

   a. What groups of people are included in this evaluation? What groups are excluded? Where do you fit?

   b. What does it mean to "are not good enough for God's glory" (v. 23)? How serious is this?

2. Read Colossians 2:13–15.

   a. What was your condition prior to coming to faith in Jesus Christ (v. 13)?

   b. List the things Jesus accomplished for you on the cross, based on this passage.

   c. According to verse 15, was the cross a victory for Jesus or a defeat? Explain how this can be.

Chapter 12 • The Hardest Thing God Ever Did

Looking Under the Stones:

1. Describe several examples of "lovebursts" you have enjoyed over the years.

2. Max writes that lovebursts remind you "that what you have is greater than what you want and that what is urgent is not

always what matters." How do lovebursts do this? Try to name a few examples from your own life where you have seen this principle at work.

3. Had the paralyzed man's friends given up when they saw the full house, what do you suppose would have happened to the man? Do you have any friends who would go as far to help you as this man's friends did for him? Are you such a friend for anyone else?

4. Max writes, "Faith does the unexpected. And faith gets God's attention." Acting in faith, have you ever done the unexpected? If so, what happened?

5. Comment on the following statement: "They want to give the man a new body so he can walk. Jesus gives grace so the man can live." What implications does this have for our day-to-day lives?

6. Are you glad that God often bypasses our requests and gives us what we need instead? Explain.

7. Try to list at least five implications of the fact that Jesus has the authority to forgive sins.

Building on the Rock:

1. Read Mark 2:1–12.

   a. Whose faith did Jesus respond to in his healing of the paralytic (v. 5)? What significance does this have in regard to many contemporary claims of faith healings (or the failure to heal)?

   b. It is obviously as easy to say, "Stand up, take your mat, and go home," as it is to say, "Your sins are forgiven," so why did Jesus ask the question in verse 9? By healing the paralytic right after he asked this question, what point was he making? What claim was he making for himself?

2. Read Psalm 50:15.

   a. What does God instruct us to do in this verse? What does he promise to do? How are we to respond?

3. Read Romans 8:26–27 and Ephesians 3:20–21.

   a. According to Romans 8:26, how accurate are we in what we pray for? What is God's solution to our problem?

   b. How does the Ephesians passage add to this understanding of prayer? How should we respond?

Chapter 13 • What Only God Can Do

Looking Under the Stones:

1. How would you define a "legalist"? Do most legalists consider themselves as such? Explain.

2. In what way does a legalist "prepare the soil but forget the seed"? What does this picture tell us about legalism?

3. Why do you think Jesus ignored Nicodemus's comment in John 3:2 and instead responded, "I tell you the truth, unless a man is born again, he cannot be in God's kingdom"? Was this polite?

4. What does Max mean when he writes, "All the world religions can be placed in one of two camps: legalism or grace"? In which camp does your religion fall? How do you know?

5. Comment on the following statement: "Legalism is slow torture, suffocation of the spirit, amputation of the dreams." If you have ever felt legalism's grip, describe your experience.

6. Do you agree with the statement that "every spiritual achievement is created and energized by God"? Why or why not?

7. In your own words, define the term *grace* (and don't say, "God's unmerited favor"!).

8. How does John 19:39–42 prove that Nicodemus finally escaped the trap of legalism? How did he escape its grip?

Building on the Rock:

1. Read Galatians 5:1–6.

   a. What danger does Paul warn us about in this passage? Why is it a real threat?

   b. How does this passage teach that salvation cannot be achieved through a mixture of faith and deeds?

2. Read Colossians 2:20–23.

   a. What reason does Paul give in verse 20 for refusing to submit to man-made rules? What does this mean?

   b. In what way do many human regulations "have an appearance of wisdom"? What makes them attractive?

   c. How effective are our rules at restraining sensual indulgence (v. 23)?

   d. Why do you think we are so easily drawn back into legalism? What is the only way to stay free of it?

Chapter 14 • Galilean Grace

Looking Under the Stones:

1. Why do you think Peter denied the Lord after Jesus was arrested? Have you ever "denied" him in a similar way? If so, describe the situation.

2. How was Peter's denial an illustration of Proverbs 16:18? How is his experience a lesson and a warning for us?

3. Have you ever been loyal to the Lord . . . from a distance? If so, what were the circumstances surrounding this event?

4. When Luke 22:61 says that Jesus "turned and looked straight at Peter," what sort of look do you think it was? Accusing? Condemning? Compassionate? Exasperated? Sorrowful? Explain your answer.

5. How do you think Peter felt at the moment he plunged into the lake to meet the Lord on the beach? What was going through his mind?

6. Max imagines a moment after we have sinned and writes, "It's just you and God. You and God both know what you did. And neither one of you is proud of it. What do you do?" How would you answer his question?

7. Comment on the following statement: "[God] invites you to try again. This time, with him." Exactly *how* do you try something again, this time with God? What do you do differently than you tried the first time around?

Building on the Rock:

1. Read John 21:14–19.

a. The restoration of Peter was not complete until he went through the encounter described in this passage. What was Jesus trying to accomplish in this meeting? How did he do it?

b. Notice Jesus' final charge to Peter in verse 19. How is this both different and the same as his original call recorded in Matthew 4:19? How is this significant?

Chapter 15 • The Tenderness of God

Looking Under the Stones:

1. Max writes that Jesus was referring to some kind of plan when he spoke phrases such as "the time has not yet come." What plan is he speaking of? A plan to do what?

2. Max writes, "The inaugural miracle is motivated—not by tragedy or famine or moral collapse—but by concern for friends who are in a bind." What does this say about Jesus? How does this knowledge affect the way you relate to him today?

3. Comment on the statement: "This miracle tells you that what matters to you, matters to God." How true is this? How do you know? What examples from your own life can you produce to demonstrate its truth?

4. How do you think God sees you? If he were to describe you to an angel, what would he say? What does he think of you?

5. How does Denalyn's response to her daughter Jenna illustrate how God responds to the pain of his own children?

6. Jesus' first miracle was turning water into wine at the wedding of some friends; his last miracle was to heal the ear of a man who had come to arrest him (see Luke 22:50–51). What does this tell you about Jesus' availability to listen to your requests?

Building on the Rock:

1. Read Hebrews 4:14–16.

   a. How is Jesus described in this passage? List each description.

   b. Based on the characteristics listed above, what should be our response? What are we encouraged to do?

2. Read Philippians 4:6–7.

   a. What things does this text instruct us to pray for? What elements of prayer does it mention?

   b. According to verse 7, what results can we expect from praying as we are instructed in verse 6?

3. Read 1 Peter 5:6–7.

   a. What are we instructed to do in verse 6? How do you do this? What promise is given?

   b. How is verse 7 dependent upon verse 6? What are we told to do in verse 7? What promise is given?

Chapter 16 • The Madman Turned Missionary

Looking Under the Stones:

1. Were you surprised to learn that the first missionary was a former lunatic? Explain your answer.

2. Max writes, "Jesus' mere appearance humbles the demons. Though they had dominated this man, they cower before God." How should this be a tremendous encouragement to us today?

3. The demons implore Jesus to send them into a herd of swine, and Jesus does so. But why would the demons make such a request if they immediately drove the pigs to their death? (See John 8:44; 10:10.) What does this tell you about demonic character?

4. How was a young Max able to get through the storm that threatened to capsize his fishing boat? How can we emulate his actions in regard to our relationship with our heavenly Father?

5. Max writes, "When the fighting is fierce, stand back and let the Father fight." Is this good advice? What does it mean in practical terms? How do you "stand back and let the Father fight"?

6. Why do you think the people asked Jesus to leave their territory after he had delivered the demoniac? Raw fear? Fear of change? Fear of further economic loss?

7. When Jesus told the formerly demon-possessed man to go home to his family and tell them how much God had done for him, it was one of the few times he instructed someone to broadcast the news of a healing. What was different in this man's case? Why did Jesus tell this man to testify, but the others to keep quiet (see Mark 1:40–45)?

Building on the Rock:

1. Read 1 Corinthians 15:8–11 and 1 Timothy 1:12–16.

   a. Why was Paul amazed that God called him to be a missionary? According to these passages, what were his credentials?

   b. According to 1 Timothy 1:16, why did God choose Paul to be an apostle? What does this suggest for you and me?

2. Read 2 Corinthians 10:3–5.

a. What insight does this passage give us into fighting in the spiritual realm?

b. How does this passage show that the only way to win the fight is by resting in the Father's strength?

Chapter 17 • Seeing the Unseen

Looking Under the Stones:

1. What did you think of Max's "faith experiment" with his daughters? What was he trying to teach them?

2. Do you ever wish you could see into the future? What would be the benefits of doing so? The drawbacks? If you could acquire the ability to see your whole future, would you do so? Explain.

3. Max writes, "There are times in life when everything you have to offer is nothing compared to what you are asking to receive." Describe a time in your life when this was true of you.

4. Have you ever tried to "barter" with the Lord? ("You do this for me and I'll . . .") What's wrong with bartering? Why isn't God at all interested in it?

5. Max claims that a critical principle for seeing the unseen is to ignore what people say. What does he mean? What sort of people do you ignore? What kinds of advice do you refuse to heed? Couldn't Max's advice be dangerous in some circumstances? In what kind of circumstances?

6. Comment on the concentration camp inmate's words: "I believe in the sun, even though it doesn't shine, I believe in love, even when it isn't shown, I believe in God, even when he doesn't speak." Do you have faith like this? Explain your answer.

7. Max writes, "Death is a small price to pay for the privilege of sitting at [God's] table." Do you agree with him? Why or why not?

8. Why did Jesus throw the people out of Jairus's home?

9. What did you learn about faith from Max's experiment with his daughters?

Building on the Rock:

1. Read 1 Corinthians 15:50–57.

   a. According to this passage, why cannot "flesh and blood" inherit the kingdom of God?

   b. What must occur for us to take our place at God's side? Who makes it possible for us to get there (v. 57)? How did he do this?

2. Read 2 Corinthians 4:16–18.

   a. What reason does Paul give in verse 16 for not giving up hope? How does he amplify this in verse 17?

   b. According to verse 18, how permanent is the world we see? How permanent is the world we do not see? How do you "Set our eyes" on Jesus?

Chapter 18 • Joseph's Prayer

Looking Under the Stones:

1. What questions do you have that were prompted by the Bible's silence?

2. What do you imagine Joseph thought about in the stable while Jesus was being born? If your guess is different from Max's, describe it.

3. Describe a time when you were caught between what God says and what seemed to make sense.

4. What does it mean to you to walk by faith, not by sight? How can you know for sure that you're on the right trail?

5. What is the connection between our obedience and divine guidance. Why is it pointless to ask God for direction for your life if you are disobeying some command of Scripture?

6. What instances in your past have caused you to question why God did what he did?

7. What generally happens to your attitude when you question God's handling of your life or circumstances? Is there a pattern you can discern?

8. How do you respond to Max's question: "Will you serve . . . even when you don't understand?"

Building on the Rock:

1. Read Hebrews 3:12–19.

   a. What advice is given in verse 13 to help us obey God together?

   b. Note the close connection between obedience and belief in verses 18 and 19. What is this connection?

2. Read 1 Samuel 15:22–23.

a. Samuel delivered this speech to Saul after the king had disobeyed a direct divine command. To what does Samuel contrast obedience in verse 22? Which of these two things does God treasure the most?

b. To what does Samuel compare disobedience? What were the consequences for Saul's disobedience?

3. Read Job 42:1–6.

a. When Job comes face to face with God, what happens to his questions?

b. When Job finally gets a clear picture of God, how does he respond? How does the story end in 42:7–17? How is this important?

Chapter 19 • The Grave Fact

Looking Under the Stones:

1. How often do you think of death? What images does it create in your mind?

2. Describe what you felt and did the first time a loved one died.

3. As you get older, do you find yourself thinking more about death? Do you ever try to imagine your own funeral? If so, describe it.

4. How does death "unearth our view of God"?

5. Have you ever found yourself thinking or saying something like, "If you were doing your part, God, my husband would have survived." "If you'd done what was right, Lord, my baby would have lived"? Do you know anyone who has acted in this way? How did you respond in each case?

6. Do you agree that many of us "interpret the presence of death as the absence of God"? Explain your answer.

7. Max writes that Christians serve "the kind of God who rolls back the sleeve of the trickster and reveals death for the parlor trick it is." What does he mean? What hope can this give you?

Building on the Rock:

1. Read 1 Thessalonians 4:13–18.

   a. According to this passage, why are Christians not to grieve like the unbelieving world? What hope do Christians have that unbelievers don't?

   b. What promise is given in verse 17? How is this to encourage us?

2. Read John 14:1–3.

   a. What is the bedrock way to remove the fear of death, according to verse 1?

   b. What is the tremendous promise given to every believer in verses 2–3? How can this give us courage in the face of death?

3. Read Revelation 21:1–7, 9–22:5.

   a. List as many characteristics of our final home as you can find in this passage.

   b. For you personally, what is the greatest promise contained in this passage?

Chapter 20 • Listless Christianity

Looking Under the Stones:

1. Do most of your friends and acquaintances believe in heaven? What do they think it's like?

2. How do most of the people you know believe someone "makes it" to heaven? What is on their "list"?

3. What is on *your* list of what it takes to get to heaven? How can you be confident that your list is accurate?

4. How did one of the thieves crucified with Jesus go so quickly from reviling the Lord to asking for a reservation in paradise? Doesn't this sound like a contradiction?

5. Max imagines that the thief thought, "I am wrong; Jesus is right. I have failed; Jesus has not. I deserve to die; Jesus deserves to live." How do these statements constitute "the core of the gospel"?

6. How do you feel about Max's conviction that, "You see, that is you and me on the cross. Naked, desolate, hopeless, and estranged. That is us"? Is this insulting or accurate? Explain your answer.

7. Do you agree that "we, like the thief, are able to endure the pain knowing he'll soon take us home"? Why or why not?

8. If in heaven you could ask the thief on the cross any question at all, what would you ask him? Why?

Building on the Rock:

1. Read Romans 10:9–13.

a. How can we enter into a life-giving relationship with God, according to this passage? What "list" does this passage give?

b. How does the thief's story stack up against this passage? Is his conversion story a good illustration of what Paul wrote here?

c. Have you ever taken the steps Paul outlines here?

2. Read 2 Corinthians 5:1–5, 17–6:2.

a. For what purpose has God made us, according to verses 4 and 5? What guarantee has he given us that he will fulfill his promise to us?

b. How is verse 21 an excellent summary of the gospel message? According to 6:1–2, how do we apply the work of Christ to our own behalf?

Chapter 21 • The Stone Mover's Gallery

Looking Under the Stones:

1. Why do you think the Bible is full of stories of hurting men and women?

2. Max writes, "The goal of these stories is not to help us look back with amazement, but forward with faith." What is the difference between the two? Describe any times when you have made this mistake. How did you correct it?

3. Take some time, as Max says, to "record your drama. Retell your saga. Plot your journey." Follow his suggestion and:

a. Begin with your experience before you knew Jesus.

b. Then describe your present experience.

c. Last, share your story with someone else.

4. If you were to pick a single item that characterizes either your salvation experience or your subsequent Christian walk, what would that thing be? Explain your choice.

5. Discuss Max's comment, "Stones were never a match for God." What stones has he removed in your own life? What stones are even now blocking your way? How does it help to remember that "stones were never a match for God"?

6. What has been the most helpful insight to you in *He Still Moves Stones?* Has anything left you a little puzzled? Spend a few moments "debriefing" your reading experience.

Building on the Rock:

1. Read 1 Corinthians 1:26 and Philippians 1:6.

   a. According to 1 Corinthians 1:26, why did Paul think it was important for the Corinthians to remember their pre-Christian lives? Is it important for us to remember our own pre-Christian lives? Why or why not?

   b. According to Philippians 1:6, what two truths help to keep us on track in our Christian lives?

2. Read Romans 15:4 and 1 Corinthians 10:11–13.

   a. According to Romans 15:4, why were so many stories of hurting people included in the Bible? What two specific reasons are given?

   b. According to 1 Corinthians 10:11–13, what other specific reasons did God have in mind when he gave us these stories in the Bible? How are these stories supposed to help us today?